BEST HIKES
WITH CHILDREN

BEST HIKES WITH CHILDREN

In Western Washington & The Cascades

Joan Burton

*Photographs by
Bob and Ira Spring*

THE MOUNTAINEERS/Seattle

The Mountaineers: Organized 1906 "...to explore, study, preserve, and enjoy the natural beauty of the Northwest."

2 1 0 9 8
5 4 3 2 1

Published by The Mountaineers
306 Second Avenue West, Seattle, Washington 98119

Published simultaneously in Canada by Douglas & McIntyre, Ltd.,
1615 Venables Street, Vancouver, B.C. V5L 2H1

Manufactured in the United States of America

Photographs by Bob and Ira Spring
Copyedited by Miriam Bulmer
Book design by Bridget Culligan
Cover design by Betty Watson
Maps by Nick Gregoric
Cover photograph: Mount Shuksan from near the Chain Lakes Trail
Frontispiece: Camping at Twin Lakes on the side of Mount Margaret

Photo credits: John Spring: pages 64, 67, 70, 72, 75, 79, 80, 93, 94, 97, 132; Harvey Manning: page 125; Marge and Ted Mueller: pages ii, 56, 76, 192

LIBRARY OF CONGRESS
Library of Congress Cataloging-in-Publication Data

Burton, Joan, 1935-
    Best hikes with children in western Washington & the Cascades / Joan Burton; photography by Bob and Ira Spring.
    p.   cm.
    Bibliography: p.
    Includes index.
    ISBN 0-89886-179-9 (pbk.)
    1. Hiking — Washington (State) — Guide-books.   2. Hiking — Cascade Range — Guide-books.   3. Family recreation — Northwest, Pacific — Guide-books.   4. Washington (State) — Description and travel — 1981 — Guide-books.   5. Cascade Range — Description and travel — Guide-books.
I. Spring, Bob, 1918-   .   II: Spring, Ira.   III. Title.
GV199.42.W2B87   1988
917.97 — dc19
                                                    88-23463
                                                    CIP
                                                    (Rev.)

CONTENTS

Acknowledgments...Page 4

Foreword...Page 5

Introduction...Page 7

Mount Baker Highway *(State Route 542)*

Hikes 1-4...Pages 16-25

North Cascade Highway *(State Route 20)*: West

Hikes 5-12...Pages 26-43

North Cascade Highway *(State Route 20)*: East

Hikes 13-17...Pages 44-55

Mountain Loop Highway *(State Routes 92 and 530)*

Hikes 18-30...Pages 56-83

Stevens Pass Highway *(U.S. 2)*: West

Hikes 31-38...Pages 84-101

Stevens Pass Highway *(U.S. 2)*: East/

Chelan Highway *(U.S. 97)*

Hikes 39-46...Pages 102-119

Snoqualmie Pass Highway *(Interstate 90)*: West

Hikes 47-53...Pages 120-135

Snoqualmie Pass Highway *(Interstate 90)*: East

Hikes 54-57...Pages 136-145

Chinook Pass Highway *(U.S. 410)*: West

Hikes 58-63...Pages 146-159

Chinook Pass Highway *(U.S. 410)*: East

Hikes 64-69...Pages 160-173

Mount Rainier National Park Highway *(State Route 760)*

Hikes 70-77...Pages 174-191

White Pass Highway *(State Route 12)*

Hikes 78-81...Pages 192-201

Southern Cascade Highways

(State Routes 12, 503, 14, and 141)

Hikes 82-90...Pages 202-221

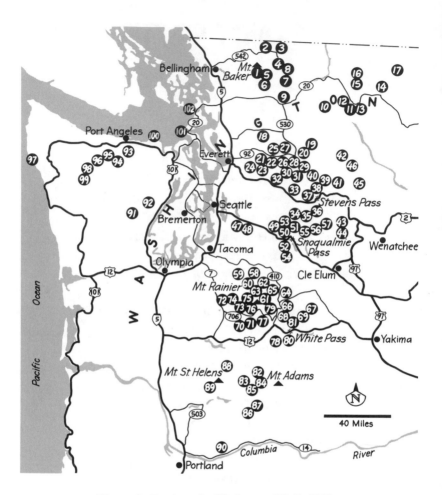

Olympic Peninsula Highway *(U.S. 101)*
Hikes 91-100...Pages 222-243
Whidbey Island Highway *(State Route 20)*
Hikes 101-102...Pages 244-249
Index...Page 250

KEY TO SYMBOLS

 Dayhikes. These are hikes that can be completed in a single day. While most trips allow camping, few require it.

 Backpack trips. These are hikes whose length or difficulty makes camping out either necessary or recommended for most families.

 Easy trails. These are relatively short, smooth, gentle trails suitable for small children or first-time hikers.

 Moderate trails. Most of these are 2 to 4 miles total distance and feature more than 500 feet of elevation gain. The trail may be rough and uneven. Hikers should wear lug-soled boots and be sure to carry the Ten Essentials (see below).

 Difficult trails. These are often rough, with considerable elevation gain or distance to travel. They are suitable for older or experienced children. Lug-soled boots and the Ten Essentials are standard equipment.

 Hikable. The best times of year to hike each trail are indicated by the following symbols: flower — spring; sun — summer; leaf — fall; snowflake — winter.

 Driving directions. These paragraphs tell you how to get to the trailheads.

 Turnarounds. These are places, mostly along moderate or difficult trails, where families can cut their hike short yet still have a satisfying outing. Turnarounds usually offer picnic opportunities, views, or special natural attractions.

 Cautions. These mark potential hazards — cliffs, stream crossings, and the like — where close supervision of children is strongly recommended.

LEGEND

Interstate Highway			Boundary
U.S. Highway		• or ▥	Towns
State Highway			Ranger Station
			Lookout
Forest Roads			Campsite
Parking			Viewpoint
Trail			Falls
Trail continues on			

ACKNOWLEDGMENTS

For his constant help, encouragement, willingness to check trail and road maps, and loyal support, I wish to thank Ira Spring.

John Spring scouted and double-checked many of the hikes.

Jerry Franklin advised me and gave me help with ecological information.

Harvey Manning read the whole manuscript twice and made many helpful suggestions.

I feel fortunate to have such knowledgeable good friends.

Joan Burton

Foreword

When I heard my father (Ira Spring) was doing the photographs for a children's hiking guide, I was thrilled. I consider my father and my mother to be bona fide experts on the subject. They took me on my first hike when I was five months old, taught me to hike the same day I learned to walk, kept me interested when I was a teenager, and encouraged me to set out on my own as an adult.

It has been quite a few years since I was a little child, trailing along after my parents, walking through rain storms and crying because I was promised two nights out in the snow and only got one. However, I still remember my feelings when I had short legs and everybody else had long ones.

Hiking was fun because my parents told me it was fun, and I was a very trusting child. And my parents worked to make it fun for me. First, we always had a destination. I knew when my feet hit the trail how far I had to go, and woe and misfortune to anyone who suggested that we should turn back before reaching some wonderful lake, the tiptop of a real, but probably quite small mountain or, best of all, an old lookout site that was sure to be strewn with treasures.

Second, I always had the company of my older brother, and maybe a cousin or a friend. This was very clever of my parents because we competed with each other to see who could go the fastest the longest. By myself, with just my two parents for company, I would have gotten bored and quickly become exhausted.

Third, my parents always carried incredible treats whenever we hiked. At home we never were given big chunks of chocolate, or any kind of candy at all, that I can remember. However, on the trail they carried "energy food" and, believe me, my brother and I fell for that trick quite happily. "Five more switchbacks and we take an energy stop" would have us running up the trail as fast as we could.

There are a lot of unpleasant things about hiking that bother little children. My parents took care to make sure that these things did not ruin our experience. They wanted us to want to go hiking again, so we were not asked to become macho woodsmen overnight. I can remember being carried on my father's shoulders through nettle patches, being lifted over logs, being taught to make slapping mosquitos a game, and being fed dinner in a warm tent when it was raining.

As soon as we were old enough, my parents liberated my brother and me. We were allowed to go ahead as long as we stuck together and stayed on the trail. This was the best. Together we never had time to be tired. Our first aim was to get as far ahead of our parents as possible. Then we proceeded to have a great time, playing at being motorcycles, trucks, or race cars as we zoomed up the switchbacks.

Looking back, I would say that my parents' most effective ploy was to have only one daypack for my brother and me. When my brother realized that he was to have the pack and I wasn't, he was very proud and I was green with jealousy. They dumped pounds of stuff in that pack and still my brother carried it, just because he knew how badly I wanted to. And, can you believe this? As soon as as my parents let us go ahead, he would let me carry it for miles as long as I promised not to tell! It wasn't until I was nine and had read *Tom Sawyer* that I finally caught on, and my parents had to buy me a pack of my very own to get me to carry anything.

Maybe the most important thing my parents did was never to complain in my hearing. If the trail was bad, if they were cold, tired, or just out of sorts, we never knew it. My parents were excellent role models on the trail. I really didn't know it was okay to complain when things were really bad. After all I had never heard them complain.

One day my mother nearly got sick when she saw me pull off my socks, bloodstained almost to the ankles from bleeding blisters. This was really unfortunate, because the best thing about hiking was that it got my brother and me out of doing our mandatory four hours of work around the house before we were set free to play. So you can understand that I was devastated when my mother decided that I would have to stay home until the blisters on my feet healed to *her* satisfaction. I got blisters on my hands from working in the garden before I was allowed back on the trail with new boots.

Now that I am grown up, carry a heavier pack than my parents, and sometimes slow down enough to hike with them, I'm not sure if being given a taste for the outdoors was a good thing. By the time I was a teenager I was hooked on the outdoors; now I'm addicted. My house is filled with tents, skis, hiking boots, climbing ropes, and bicycles. And holding a steady job is not to my taste at all. Rather than sit at some old desk, I would much rather tighten my belt, load up the pack, and head for the outdoors whenever I want. It's all my parents' fault....

Vicky Spring
Former Kid

Introduction

Hiking with little children requires planning, patience, psychology, strategy, and, at some points, outright bribery. Is it worth it? Of course it is! You, the parents, can introduce them to the outdoors, have some "family time," and hike to places you've wanted to see anyway. With luck they may grow up to love the mountains, rivers, lakes, and beaches, and be willing to carry their own packs.

Read on for some of the strategies that worked with my children when they were young, susceptible, and believed everything I told them.

1. **Appoint a "First Leader."** I rotated this official designation among my three children. Somehow, being tagged "First Leader" imparted status — and extra energy, at least for awhile. Unspoken competition between brothers and sisters can be a powerful motivating force (which is why we did not encourage walking sticks). It's a good idea to agree in advance on a point at which the official title rotates again.

2. **Frequent "energy stops."** As in, "When we get to that creek ahead, we'll need to have an energy stop, where we'll have some..."

3. **"Energy food."** Candy, fruit, or a favorite family treat. Never *called* candy, and always rationed out in tiny increments to prolong its effectiveness. Popeye's spinach comes to mind.

4. **Take a friend along.** Aches, pains, and complaints are often forgotten when there is a companion the child's own age along on the hike. The child will not want to look slow or tired in front of the friend, and a little friendly rivalry, not unlike sibling rivalry, won't hurt.

5. **Praise, praise, praise.** Only a parent knows how thick to spread this, but positive reinforcement may have the most durable results of all. When my sister and I were eight and nine, my father took us to Melakwa Lake. Over 40 years later I still remember what a fuss he made over how strong and fast we were. His praise was probably vast exaggeration, but consider the effect it had.

6. **Patience.** This means taking time, if necessary, to inspect every creek, throw sticks and stones over bridges, look up for birds, and down at animal tracks. If parents want to get home (or into a campsite) before dark, they must plan ahead for a pace to fit the child's ability and attention span. Try not to look at your watch any more than necessary. If you keep winding it and shaking it, the child will suspect you are not having as much fun as he or she is.

HOW TO USE THIS BOOK

Most of the hikes described in this guidebook are in the Cascade Range or the Olympic Mountains. A few are found in nearby foothills and lowlands. The hikes are numbered consecutively but grouped by the major highways from which they are accessible. This arrangement makes it easy for readers to find the hikes they want. See the table of contents for a complete list of hikes by highway.

Each hike description includes (1) a block summarizing important information about each hike, (2) symbols for features of special interest, and (3) the description itself, which tells you what to expect, how to get to the trail, and where to go from there.

Hikes are rated easy, moderate, or difficult. These ratings are only approximations. I tried to factor in distances, elevation gains, and trail conditions, but even those are not altogether objective criteria. I thought of giving minimum age levels for trails, but found that to be even more subjective. A trail one five-year-old is capable of hiking may be too difficult for another. In any case, the most important factor is motivation. If kids want to hike somewhere, energy and stamina will follow; the reverse is also true. If children do not want to go on, any trail at any time can be too steep and too long.

The great majority of hikes can be completed in one day, but camping opportunities are plentiful and have been noted for families who are more adventurous or experienced. Some trips are primarily overnight excursions, but beginning sections can make good dayhikes; it is not always necessary to walk the entire distance.

In the same way, many hikes that are rated *moderate* or *difficult* contain shorter, easier sections that make excellent dayhikes in their own right. So if you want a shorter outing, don't restrict your search only to those hikes that I have rated *easy*. Instead, scan the more difficult trips for what I call "turnarounds," which are marked in both margin and text by a special symbol (see "Key to Symbols" below). Turnarounds are satisfying destinations that make fine picnic spots and feature scenic views or other natural attractions. You can turn around at a turnaround and feel well satisfied with your hike.

I have also indicated the months during which each trail is free of snow. This can vary from year to year. Early or late in the season, when there may be some doubt about current snow conditions, call the local ranger station in the area where you want to hike.

Hikers venturing into wild or otherwise roadless areas should carry a topographic map and compass (most outdoor-equipment stores stock them) and know how to use them. Green Trails topographic maps and U.S. Forest Service or National Park Service maps are listed for each hike.

Maps

Topographic maps show terrain and altitude by means of contour lines and provide a fairly accurate way of gauging trail steepness and general terrain features. The Green Trails maps are one of two types of topographic maps widely used by local hikers. The second type is published by the United States Geologic Survey (USGS). Though widely available, many USGS maps are out of date, and they do not give recent road or trail numbers. Green Trails maps are listed because they are updated more often and show all existing trails in green, features which are particularly important for beginning hikers.

An appropriate U.S. Forest Service or National Park Service map is also listed for each hike. These maps generally do not show contours, but they do give the names and numbers of all access roads, which no other types of map do. This is particularly important for hikers venturing into an area for the first time.

Numbering of National Forest roads has become rather complicated. Major forest roads are identified by two- or four-digit numbers, but those designating minor roads may have seven digits. In such numbers the first three digits indicate the main road, the remainder, a particular spur leading off the main one. Be sure the map you carry is as up to date as possible.

Road mileage is expressed in decimals rounded to the nearest tenth of a mile to correspond to odometer readings. Trail mileage is expressed in fractions because decimals imply a greater degree of accuracy than is possible or practical on trails. Even so, all mileages are as accurate as possible.

WHAT TO TAKE

Boots

Rocky, uneven trails can subject small feet and shoes alike to more wear and tear than they are designed to handle. On many of the shorter, gentler trails in this book running shoes or other sneakers may be adequate, but on longer, steeper trails, or when carrying a heavy pack, such footwear may not offer enough protection. Boots are a must for extended dayhikes and all backpack trips. Unfortunately, boots for children are expensive — especially since children's feet somehow seem to grow even faster than the rest of them. But there's hope for the budget. I bought one pair of good boots for the first child, passed them down the line, and traded around outgrown hand-me-downs with other families. Some outdoor-equipment stores will take back usable children's boots for their rental trade and offer a price based on their value, which can be applied to the next pair.

In buying boots (for children or adults), keep in mind that boots that don't fit properly can make their owner utterly miserable (so can wet tennis shoes). It is therefore important to make sure your child's boots fit properly. They should be snug enough to prevent chafing but not so tight that they pinch toes. After buying your child a pair of boots, have him or her wear them inside the house for several days before using them outdoors. This will not only help to break in the boots but will often reveal poorly fitting ones while it's still possible to return them. Usually, an ill-fitting pair can be returned for full value. Even well-fitting boots, however, need to be broken in before they are suitable for an extended hike. Otherwise, blisters are virtually certain. For that reason, children forced to hike far in stiff new boots may never willingly hike anywhere again.

Packs

Child-size packs and bags are available at most backpacking stores, but parents can calculate how soon they will be outgrown and how much use they will get. Sometimes, packs are a source of rivalry among little children, who are likely to gauge another child's load by size alone. Unless a child has his or her own pack, good parental strategy is to fill an adult daypack with the child's extra clothing, take a tuck in the straps, and allow him or her to appear to be carrying an enormous load. This is a sure-fire morale booster for a kid. Other children on the trail are not likely to heft one another's packs, so no one but the parents will know how much is in it.

The Ten Essentials

Over the years, The Mountaineers has compiled a list of ten items that should be taken on *every* hike. These "Ten Essentials" not only make your trip more comfortable but equip you to cope with emergencies caused by bad weather, injury, or other unforeseen circumstances.

1. **Extra clothing.** Weather changes or an unplanned swim mean trouble if there are no changes of clothing.

2. **Extra food.** Carry enough food so that if your hike lasts longer

than you expect, you and your children won't be hungry.

3. **Sunglasses.** Bright sun on snow or water can be blinding.

4. **Knife.** Useful in countless situations.

5. **Firestarter-candle or chemical fuel.** If you should unexpectedly have to stay overnight, you will want to build a fire.

6. **First-aid kit.** Keep it well supplied and hope you won't need it.

7. **Matches in a waterproof container.** No fire is possible without them. Look for waterproof matches in outing stores.

8. **Flashlight.** Imagine walking down a trail in the dark with little children — without a light.

9. **Map.** Be sure you have the correct and current map for your hike.

10. **Compass.** Know how to use it with your map to orient yourself.

Children require a few extra essentials; the items mentioned below are ones I found useful.

Mosquitoes, no-see-ums, gnats, deerflies, and sunburn can make anyone miserable. Obviously you will need protection from insects and sun. But chemical products designed for adult skin — particularly sun creams with high screen factors — may be too harsh for children. Take the time to check and test untried products before you leave home. Don't assume they will be safe if there is even a possibility of an allergic reaction — two miles away from the car and 50 miles from home is no place to find out.

Be sure each child has a long-sleeved shirt to wear when bugs attack. There may even be times when a cap, gloves, and long pants will be needed. Repellent helps some but is overrated. Give the kids (and yourselves) personal "habitats" — a six-foot length of no-see-um netting for each camper, light enough to wad up in a pocket, large enough to cover the head and be tucked under the bottom at dinner time. If your child is allergic to bee or wasp stings, be sure to carry the appropriate medications prescribed or recommended by your physician.

Your first-aid kit should also contain any other special medicines or supplies your child may need, such as extra moleskin for blisters on tender feet, extra toilet paper, and some baking soda to plaster on nettle or other stings.

Do not encourage children to go into lakes in jeans, because wet jeans can become extremely cold and uncomfortable later when walking out. Carry shorts or bathing suits for wading and swimming. Also, hidden hazards lie on lake bottoms. Carry an extra pair of tennis shoes for the child to wade in, to protect him or her from sharp rocks and sticks buried in muddy lake bottoms.

Food

Food is a matter of family preference, of course. My family enjoyed meals whose ingredients came from the grocery store rather than those with freeze-dried foods from sporting goods shops. Freeze-dried foods are not only more expensive, but also less tasty than familiar home favorites. Don't experiment with unknown, gourmet foods on a camping trip with children. Comfort foods are one-pot meals — such as stew, chili, chicken and noodles, etc. — that children know from home. Dayhike foods should be combinations of nuts, fruit, candies, raisins, cheese, and crackers that are easy to carry without being crushed in the pack, and impart energy.

Safety

Backcountry travel, even on dayhikes, entails unavoidable risks that every hiker assumes and must be aware of and respect. The fact that a trail is described in this book is not a representation that it will be safe for you. The trips presented here vary in difficulty and in the amount and kind of preparation needed to enjoy them safely. Some routes may have changed, or conditions on them may have deteriorated since this book was written. Also, of course, especially in mountain areas, conditions can change even from day to day, owing to weather and other factors. A trip that is safe in good weather or for a well-conditioned, properly equipped hiker may be completely unsafe for someone else, or unsafe for anyone in adverse weather.

You can minimize your risks by being knowledgeable, prepared, and alert. There is not space in this book for a general treatise on wilderness safety, but there are a number of good books and public courses on the subject, and you should take advantage of them to increase your knowledge. Just as important, you should always be aware of your own limitations and conditions existing when and where you are traveling. If conditions are dangerous, or if you are not prepared to deal with them safely, change your plans! It is better to have wasted a few days than to be the subject of a wilderness rescue.

These warnings are not intended to keep you out of the wilderness. Most people enjoy safe trips through the backcountry every year. However, one element of the beauty, freedom, and excitement of the wilderness is the presence of risks that do not confront us at home. When you travel in the backcountry, you assume those risks. They can be met safely, but only if you exercise your own independent good judgment and common sense.

Water

Drinking water is another cause for concern and preparation. Do not trust that streams and lakes will supply you with pure water. Most mountain water is safe, but much is not, and there's no way to tell. If the trail is popular and the lake is crowded, be suspicious. Carry a canteen or plastic bottle of water or flavored drinks for the trail. (If you carry in cans of juice or pop, be sure to carry out empties.) Cooking water must be boiled at least 20 minutes. Iodine tablets or water filtering devices also guarantee pure water.

Hypothermia

Most of the mountain lakes described here are very cold, and weather conditions in the mountains can change abruptly. Parents should be aware of the hazards of hypothermia and carry extra clothing, and perhaps a Thermos of cocoa or hot soup. Because of their relatively small body size, little children are vulnerable to hypothermia sooner than adults exposed to the same conditions. In fact, a parent may not even recognize the symptoms in children. Children with first-stage hypothermia can be listless, whiny, and unwilling to cooperate, long before physical signs, like shivering, start to appear. Since these symptoms can also occur on hikes when children are only tired, bored, or hungry, it is important to rule out hypothermia before assuming some other cause. Early morning, late afternoon and evening, and periods of cool, overcast weather are times to be particularly alert to your child's behavior and to take immediate steps to rewarm him or her if appropriate.

GOOD OUTDOOR MANNERS

Hiking families have an obligation to teach children good outdoor manners. The hiker's motto should be "Leave trails and campsites as clean or cleaner than you found them." Parents can set an example by cleaning up someone else's messy camp and carrying out or burning leftover trash. Do not leave old plastic tarps behind for the next camping family. They blow around, are quickly ripped and tattered, and add to the litter. In fact, anything you can carry in, you can carry out. Think about how your family feels at seeing old tin cans, bottles, and plastic containers in places they have hiked miles to see.

Tell children they must not drop candy or gum wrappers, orange peels, or peanut or egg shells. These things take a long time to break down, and petrified orange peels are not an archaeological find we want to leave to posterity. Also, don't bury garbage; it doesn't stay covered for long.

Carry out cans, aluminum foil, and disposable diapers. One way to handle such materials in parents' packs is to include several zippable plastic bags for garbage, wet clothing, and the things children find along the way that they want to bring home.

Teach your children to dispose of toilet paper properly. Burying it with their stools used to be acceptable, but little creatures dig up the paper and strew it about. I've seen campsites so littered with toilet paper, the prospect of camping there was disgusting. If the family has a campfire, burn toilet paper or put it in plastic bags and pack it out. Parents should check their children's toilet area after use, to be sure they have the technique down and the area is usable by the next visitors.

Dogs are permitted, but not welcomed, on national forest trails. They are absolutely not allowed in national parks. Though childen may love dayhiking with their pet, its presence in a backpacking campsite may impact birds and small animals and annoy other campers, who came partly to get away from domestic animals.

You should know that theft, both in camps and from parked cars at trailheads, has become a major problem. So many hikers' cars have been vandalized that wise hikers arrange to be dropped off and picked up from trailheads. If you must leave a parked car for several days, don't tempt thieves by leaving expensive clothing and gear in plain view. Tell a Forest Service official, if you can, that you will be parked at such-and-such a trailhead for a duration of time, and you would appreciate having someone check your car during patrols of the area.

PARENTAL ATTITUDES

Children take their cue from grown-ups about how safe and non-threatening the woods and mountains are. If their parents are comfortable hiking in diverse places and weather conditions, the children usually feel secure and comfortable too. That is not to say you might not have some perfectly horrid experiences. My youngest cut a tooth in the middle of the night once and cried incessantly while we hiked out, reached the car, and drove almost a hundred miles home.

My daughter Carol says she remembers riding piggyback or in a forerunner of today's child carrier and putting her hands over my eyes because it was fun when I would stop and say I couldn't see. She also remembers untreated boots and soaking clothes that got wet and cold in the rain and on the wet brush alongside the path when she was First Leader.

On the other hand, we did have some triumphs. As a family recreational activity, hiking became an important way to give my children a sense of their ability to succeed at difficult but satisfying undertakings. One dayhike that gave my two younger children, at 12 and 13, a real sense of achievement was the trail to Camp Muir. I do not recommend this hike for little children. It is steep, arduous, long, and, in a fog, treacherous. But on a beautiful, windy day in late July, we started up from Paradise with boots, daypacks, and wind gear. The kids knew my husband and I had each climbed Mount Rainier, and that this was the way to the climbers' high camp.

Five hours went by — all spent switchbacking up steep snow, the guide hut always receding, like a mirage, before us. The children were weary and discouraged at how far and how steep the hike was turning out to be. We developed an unspoken unity of purpose. We were going to make Camp Muir — together. Dick, my son, would go ahead for awhile, then wait for us. Carol, who was small but wiry, would lag behind, discouraged, then surge ahead. We talked about what the summit climb is like, and the kids said later that those conversations and the collective family pride in achievement meant much to them. They knew that sometime, somehow, we were going to make it.

When we finally climbed over the Muir rocks to the coffin-shaped nests there, the wind was fierce. We hunkered down in a nest to escape the wind, and ate our lunch, rejoicing. The kids had met an important test successfully. What better gifts can parents give than self-sufficiency and self-confidence?

Camping at Artists Point near Mount Baker

Mount Baker Highway

State Route 542

1. Heliotrope Ridge...18
2. Excelsior Mountain...20
3. Twin Lakes — Winchester Mountain...22
4. Chain Lakes...24

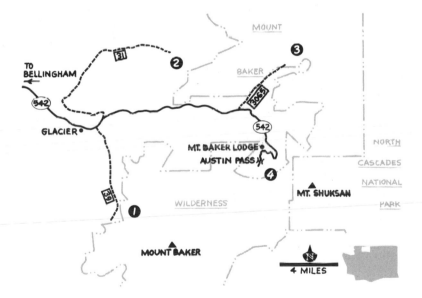

1. Heliotrope Ridge

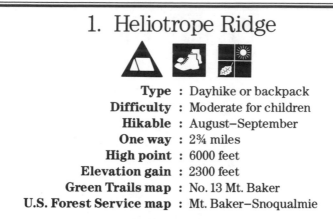

Type	:	Dayhike or backpack
Difficulty	:	Moderate for children
Hikable	:	August–September
One way	:	2¾ miles
High point	:	6000 feet
Elevation gain	:	2300 feet
Green Trails map	:	No. 13 Mt. Baker
U.S. Forest Service map	:	Mt. Baker–Snoqualmie

A child's chance to glimpse alpine wonders — to see a glacier headwall and its savage crevasses, and to hear the groaning and cracking sounds of an icefall on a shoulder of Mount Baker. Many summit climbers use this route, so children may admire them at close range as well. While experienced hikers travel this route from early July, three creek crossings are very difficult during the high-water periods of snow melt, so it is best to wait until late summer to take children.

Drive north on I-5 past Bellingham to Exit 255, then east on Mount

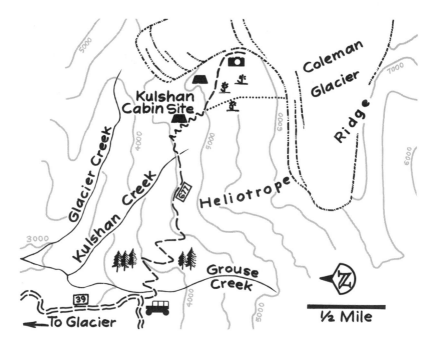

Coleman Glacier

Baker Highway 542 to the town of Glacier. About 1 mile beyond, turn right on Glacier Creek road No. 39 and follow it 8 miles to the trailhead parking lot, elevation 3700 feet.

The rough, well-used trail gains 1000 feet in 2 switchbacking miles. At 1¾ miles you cross the first difficult streams. At 2 miles you pass the site of the old Kulshan Cabin and break out of timber into open meadows and all-summer snowfields at the beginning of Heliotrope Ridge. In ¾ mile more is a young moraine overlooking the Coleman Glacier, elevation 6000 feet.

Coleman Glacier has been advancing in recent years — that is, the ice from high on the mountain is pushing down faster than the warm air at lower elevations can melt it. The aggressive Coleman frequently obliges visitors by putting on some sort of show. And even if it doesn't stage a noisy avalanche or icefall or spectacular panorama of broken crevasses, the marmots and pikas whistling messages to their families can be depended on. Look for marmot burrows, where they retreat for safety and where they hibernate, usually from September to April. Pikas like rockslides, rather than burrows. These small members of the rabbit family spend the winter in rockslides, nibbling on the hay they gathered and cured the previous summer. Scan rockslides for "cony haystacks," of succulent meadow plants left to cure in the sun.

The ridge has several possible campsites if you want to stay.

Mount Baker from the Excelsior Mountain trail

2. Excelsior Mountain

Type	:	Dayhike or backback
Difficulty	:	Moderate for children
Hikable	:	Mid-July–September
One way	:	3 miles
High point	:	5699 feet
Elevation gain	:	1200 feet
Green Trails map	:	No. 13 Mt. Baker
U.S. Forest Service map	:	Mt. Baker–Snoqualmie

My children call this the "Sound of Music Mountain" because its alpine meadows and spectacular views of Mount Baker, Mount Shuksan, and peaks across the border in Canada reminded them of the movie scenery. The mountain is actually named for a long-ago mine called the Great Excelsior. The trail is neither steep nor gentle, gaining 500 feet a mile. It can be very muddy when the snow is melting or after several days of rain.

Drive north on I-5 to Exit 255, then east on Mount Baker Highway 542 to Glacier; continue 2 miles beyond to Canyon Creek road No. 31. Turn left and drive 15 miles to the parking lot and trail No. 625, elevation 4200 feet.

Hike through lush woodland for 1 mile to a junction with the Canyon Ridge trail. Keep right and continue past the two small, marshy, but picturesque Damfino Lakes (so named because when two early travelers came here, one asked, "What lakes are these?" and the other said, "Damfino").

At 2½ miles from the road, you enter superb green meadows and cross a stream where the last drops quit flowing by mid-August. To the right are campsites without views. At 3 miles you reach Excelsior Pass, elevation 5400 feet, and the first view of Mount Baker across the deep Nooksack Valley. It is a wonderful place to have lunch, but the best is a bit farther. Either follow the trail contouring around the mountain, or take the steep, boot-beaten shortcut another ½ mile to the peak itself, 5699-foot Excelsior Mountain. Be careful not to stumble — the views are so breathtaking one may forget about feet. Mount Baker, Mount Shuksan, and the Canadian Border Peaks loom close enough that children may ask if they can stay and climb them tomorrow. In settled weather you can sleep on the summit where the fire-lookout cabin used to be. Camping here is unforgettable: imagine moonlight on two glaciated mountains, and settlement lights on the shores of Puget Sound.

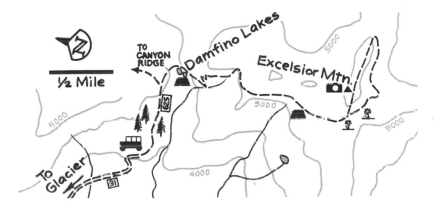

Winchester Mountain trail, Mount Shuksan in distance

3. Twin Lakes–Winchester Mountain

Type :	Backpack
Difficulty :	Moderate for children
Hikable :	August–September
One way :	2½ miles, Twin Lakes
	4 miles, Winchester Mountain
High point :	5200 feet, Twin Lakes
	6250 feet, Winchester Mountain
Elevation gain :	1600 feet, Twin Lakes
	2600 feet, Winchester Mountain
Green Trails map :	No. 14 Mt. Shuksan
U.S. Forest Service map :	Mt. Baker–Snoqualmie

This walk on an old mining road (occasionally drivable) brings families to alpine campsites at Twin Lakes, Mount Baker mirrored in their waters. Next day, follow a steep trail that ascends meadows to a historic lookout building with more views of Baker, and close-ups of many other North Cascades peaks — Shuksan, Tomyhoi, Larrabee, and the Canadian Border Peaks. Though the trail is not rough, a snowfield near the top lasts late into the summer and is steep and icy. Children should be carefully shepherded around it or turned back if no easy bypass can be found. The views here are superb already.

Drive Mount Baker Highway 542 east to Glacier and 13.5 miles beyond to the Highway Department sheds. Just past them is a sign: "Tomyhoi Trail 5, Twin Lakes 7." Turn left up narrow, steep, rough road No. 3065. At 3 miles turn left at an intersection and at 4.5 miles pass the Tomyhoi Lake trail sign. To this point the road is generally in good shape, but thereafter maintenance is intermittent and minimal; the road is an auto repairman's dream. Switchbacks are fiendishly sharp, the ruts are deep and numerous, and the rocks can run through tires like hot knives in butter. Most hikers prefer to park somewhere near the Tomyhoi Lake trailhead, elevation 3600 feet, and walk the road 2 to 2½ miles to the lakes.

Is the road-walk worth it? The first view of Twin Lakes, elevation 5200 feet, will answer the question. These two jewels are set in a cirque bowl beneath Winchester Mountain, amid subalpine trees and heather. Campers have postcard views in every direction, including a classic one of Mount Baker.

The 1½ mile Winchester trail starts between the lakes. Hike 1 mile to the High Pass trail junction and take the left fork. Climb open switchbacks through alpine gardens and late-summer blueberries. Beyond the infamous snowfield the trail becomes more gradual until you achieve the summit and its incredible views.

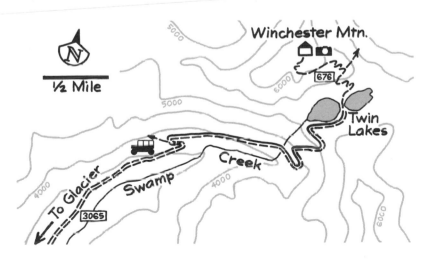

4. Chain Lakes

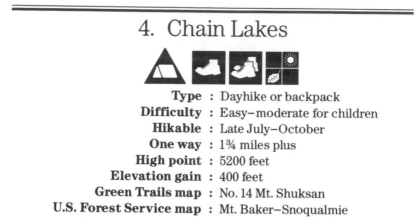

Type	:	Dayhike or backpack
Difficulty	:	Easy–moderate for children
Hikable	:	Late July–October
One way	:	1¾ miles plus
High point	:	5200 feet
Elevation gain	:	400 feet
Green Trails map	:	No. 14 Mt. Shuksan
U.S. Forest Service map	:	Mt. Baker–Snoqualmie

This group of four alpine lakes has enough scenic campsites with views to accommodate many families. If you wish, you can move camp from lake to lake along the chain and enjoy different views and different settings each day. Expect blueberries in August and September, and fish

Mazama Lake, smallest of the four Chain Lakes

in Hayes and Arbuthnot lakes anytime.

Drive east on Mount Baker Highway 542 some 60 miles from Bellingham to the Mount Baker Lodge and continue from there on a possibly snowy gravel road to its end at Kulshan Ridge, elevation 5100 feet. (The road is usually open in mid-July but some years may not thaw out until August or September.) The trailhead is to the left of the Table Mountain trail on the Mount Baker side of the parking lot.

The trail drops a few feet, then contours around the side of Table Mountain, with views of parkland meadows below and Mount Baker above. Columnar andesite formations of ancient lava flows alternate along the trail with horizontal layers of 10,000-year-old ash and pumice; those from different eruptions exhibit different colors. Tell the kids the layers are like squeezed fillings in sandwiches. They may not be impressed when you tell them much of this ash was blown out "only" 10,000 years ago, but their interest may perk up when they learn Mount Baker is thought capable of exploding again at any time, just like St. Helens.

At the highest point on the way around Table Mountain, the trail descends a steep snowfield that lasts to late summer. If there is a safe runout below, sliding may be in order, but tennis shoes will get wet.

The first of the lakes, little Mazama, is 1¾ miles. In another ¼ mile, beautiful Iceberg Lake calls to you to stop for lunch, at least. Continue on and down less than 1 mile to Hayes and Arbuthnot lakes, where some of the shores are black volcanic sand. A loop back out to the road from here is possible but is not recommended for children, so turn around and retrace your steps.

Raccoon

North Cascade Highway: West

State Route 20

5. Railroad Grade...28
6. Blue Lake...30
7. Anderson — Watson Lakes...32
8. Baker River...34
9. Sauk Mountain...36
10. Cascade Pass...38
11. Lake Ann...40
12. Heather Pass...42

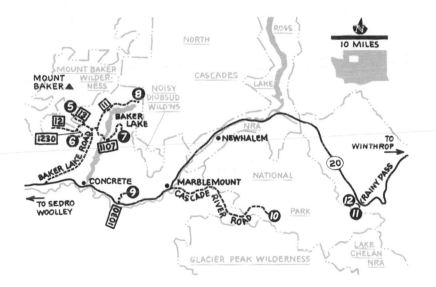

5. Railroad Grade

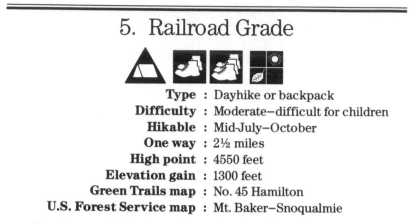

Type :	Dayhike or backpack
Difficulty :	Moderate–difficult for children
Hikable :	Mid-July–October
One way :	2½ miles
High point :	4550 feet
Elevation gain :	1300 feet
Green Trails map :	No. 45 Hamilton
U.S. Forest Service map :	Mt. Baker–Snoqualmie

The fascinating ramble from subalpine meadows up to a moraine of the Easton Glacier will delight older children. Families may stop and camp at any point along the way to enjoy views of Mount Baker, and, in season, pick blueberries.

Drive North Cascade Highway 20 east 14.5 miles past Sedro Woolley and turn left on the Baker Lake Road, passing Grandy Lake. At 12.5 miles from Highway 20, just beyond the Rocky Creek bridge, turn left on road No. 12 and go 3 miles to a junction. Go right on road No. 13 for 6 miles to its end, elevation 3200 feet.

The trail begins in subalpine forest, crossing Sulphur Creek immediately, entering meadows at ⅓ mile, and passing the ruins of two old shelter cabins on the right. Blueberries and huckleberries in late August and September are superb.

Mount Baker, from Park Butte

Crossings of several creeks at 1 mile can be difficult when the snowmelt is running, turning them into torrents.

Then comes 1 mile of steep switchbacks through old-growth timber. Energy stops may be required for jelly beans, peppermints, or berries. At approximately 2½ miles the grade gentles and the trail enters large meadows with close-up views of Mount Baker and the Easton Glacier.

Campsites are numerous. For explorations go ¼ mile to a junction. The left fork climbs to the lookout on Park Butte, maintained by volunteers. The right climbs to the snout of the Easton Glacier and its parallel moraines, so neatly heaped up and with such uniform crests they appear ready to have railroad tracks emplaced on them.

6. Blue Lake

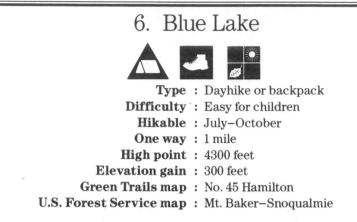

Type	: Dayhike or backpack
Difficulty	: Easy for children
Hikable	: July–October
One way	: 1 mile
High point	: 4300 feet
Elevation gain	: 300 feet
Green Trails map	: No. 45 Hamilton
U.S. Forest Service map	: Mt. Baker–Snoqualmie

Blue Lake

An easy walk to an alpine jewel of a lake. Families will find the distance and the elevation gain slight enough for young children.

Drive North Cascade Highway 20 east 14.5 miles past Sedro Woolley, turn left on the Baker Lake road 12.5 miles, and just past the Rocky Creek bridge turn left on road No. 12. Keep left at the junction with road No. 13 and at 6.6 miles from Baker Lake road turn left on road No. 1230 for another 3.8 miles to the trailhead, elevation 4000 feet.

Trail No. 604 crosses a clearcut into forest. At ⅓ mile stay left at a junction; the right fork goes to Dock Butte. The path wanders through a swamp and over roots and rocks to a cirque lake, 4000 feet. On a foggy day I almost walked right by it. The shores are lined with blueberries in late summer; fishermen claim they can get their limits in Blue Lake when they can't in Baker Lake. Families who don't want to leave can find campsites ¼ mile from the water's edge.

A short second or alternative hike is up Dock Butte, accessible by the right fork back at the second junction. The trail climbs ½ mile, past meadows, ponds, and gorgeous views. From this point the views increase, but so does the steepness. The widest views, of course, are from the old lookout site atop Dock Butte, elevation 5210 feet.

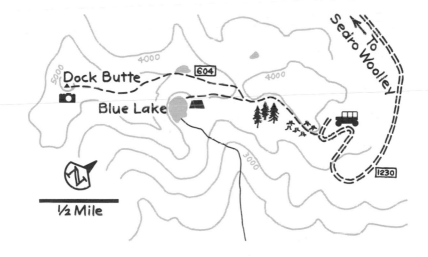

Watson Lakes

7. Anderson–Watson Lakes

Type :	Dayhike or backpack
Difficulty :	Difficult for children
Hikable :	July–October
One way :	2½ miles
High point :	4800 feet
Elevation gain :	1200 feet
Green Trails map :	No. 46 Lake Shannon
U.S. Forest Service map :	Mt. Baker–Snoqualmie

These five very popular alpine lakes are surrounded by acres of meadows, cliffs, and gorgeous scenery, and offer families diverse opportunities to camp, fish, wade, and explore. The views of Mount Baker, Mount Watson, and Anderson Butte can tempt hikers to go on and on, although trails are rough, sometimes very steep, and filled with roots and rocks.

Drive North Cascade Highway 20 east of Sedro Woolley 14.5 miles and go left on the Baker Lake–Grandy Lake Road. You enter Mount Baker Snoqualmie National Forest at 12 miles, continue approximately 2 miles more, and turn right on the Baker Dam–Baker Campground road.

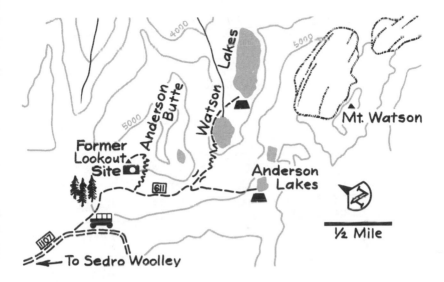

In 1 mile drive over the Baker Lake Dam (children will enjoy peering down the face of the dam to Lake Shannon below) and in 2 miles go left on gravel road No. 1107. Follow this scenic road 10 miles, savoring widening views of the lakes below, the mountains above; pass tiny Lilypad Lake before reaching the trailhead, elevation 3600 feet.

The first ⅛ mile of the trail is very steep (an omen of things to come). There are very large old-growth Douglas firs along the way, one of which has been felled and flattened on one side for 40 feet to become a part of the trail, a child's delight. The way reaches the ridge and then tilts steeply upward, sometimes on good tread and other times on roots and rock. At 1 mile pass the side trail to Anderson Butte, site of a former fire lookout. The main trail loses 100 feet and then climbs through meadows to the high point at 4700 feet before dropping steeply to a junction in about 2 miles.

Here the trail splits. The left fork climbs 150 feet over a ridge, enters the Noisy–Diobsud Wilderness, and drops steeply to more meadows and the shore of glacier-carved upper Watson Lake, 4500 feet. Lower Watson Lake, the larger of the two, is a short ¼ mile farther. Campsites here have views of the lake and of the glaciers on Bacon Peak.

The right fork is a rough, up-and-down ½ mile to Lower Anderson Lake, 4500 feet; you'll find campsites on both sides and a view of Mount Baker from the meadows. The lake is small enough, like the baby bear's chair, to be "just right" for small children.

8. Baker River

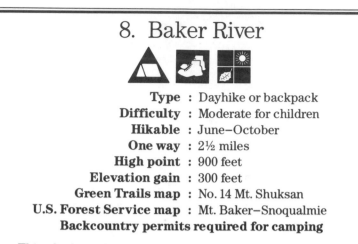

Type	:	Dayhike or backpack
Difficulty	:	Moderate for children
Hikable	:	June–October
One way	:	2½ miles
High point	:	900 feet
Elevation gain	:	300 feet
Green Trails map	:	No. 14 Mt. Shuksan
U.S. Forest Service map	:	Mt. Baker–Snoqualmie
	Backcountry permits required for camping	

This shady trail has many ups and downs as it winds through a fairyland of enormous boulders, mossy old-growth cedar trees with gnarled roots, and giant Douglas firs and western hemlocks. The trail is easy enough for a five-year-old. I met one boy with beaming eyes whose father told me he had made it round-trip the previous year. Children can

Baker River trail

look for caves under some of the boulders and for an abandoned beaver pond at 2½ miles.

Drive North Cascade Highway 20 about 14.5 miles east of Sedro Woolley and turn left on Baker Lake–Grandy Lake road. At 12 miles enter Mt. Baker–Snoqualmie National Forest and continue on, following the west side of Baker Lake. Eventually the road is designated No. 11. Near Milepost 25 go left on road No. 1168 to the road-end parking area, elevation 800 feet.

The first ½ mile of trail lies along an old road paved with riverbed boulders. The way then narrows and enters groves of ancient cedars and large maples. When these cedars were seedlings (back in the ninth century), King Alfred was fighting the Danes. Some of the boulders tumbled into position centuries ago; their mossy sides tell just how long ago that was, and they have the look of portals guarding the way. At 1½ miles is a possible sandbar camp, but the river's course changes the site every year.

A bit farther, directly below the trail, are an abandoned beaver pond and dam, built of branches and mud. When the Forest Service built the trail in the 1930s, the route went directly across the flat river bottom. Then, in the '40s, a beaver colony arrived, dammed up the side channels of the river, and flooded out the trail. Sharp eyes still can spot the puncheon of the old trail, out in the middle of the "lake." When the beavers had eaten up all the tender "salad" trees (willow, cottonwood, etc.), they emigrated. Stumps of trees near the shore show the teeth marks that felled them.

The best campsites are at the 3-mile point, where milky, glacier-fed Sulphide Creek enters the Baker River, elevation 900 feet. The water's color comes from "rock milk" — suspended ground-up rock from Sulphide Glacier high above on Mount Shuksan. When purified, it is safe to drink. The current is swift here, so go downstream for quieter pools.

9. Sauk Mountain

Type : Dayhike
Difficulty : Moderate–difficult for children
Hikable : Mid-July–October
One way : 2 miles
High point : 5537 feet
Elevation gain : 1650 feet
Green Trails map : No. 46 Lake Shannon
U.S. Forest Service map : Mt. Baker–Snoqualmie

Exposed switchbacks ascend a dizzyingly steep alpine meadow to panoramic views of Whitehorse, Baker, and Shuksan, and the merging of the serpentine Sauk and Skagit rivers. This is not a trail for toddlers, but my children loved it when they were 6, 7, and 8, and we returned to it again and again. Once one of them was bitten by a deer fly two switchbacks above me; I could hardly run uphill fast enough. She forgot about it, though, and later joyfully took her friends back up the mountain. The road goes almost to timberline, so the entire 2-mile trail is flower meadows, in season.

Drive North Cascade Highway 20 east from Concrete to the west boundary of Rockport State Park. Turn left on road No. 1030 for 8 miles of an increasingly steep grade. If the car protests, gear down, and remember, "Better the car than the hiker." At the road's end (abundant parking space), elevation 3900 feet, you may gasp at the view of the upper Skagit Valley, rivers, and North Cascades peaks.

The trail drops a bit from the parking area, then reels off 28 switchbacks (have the children count them — I might have missed a couple) up the super-steep slope. Watch carefully for hikers on the switchbacks above; some skip about as if alone in the world, kicking loose rocks that can come down like cannonballs. Also watch carefully to keep on the trail — thick grass and foliage obscure the edge and it is possible to step through flowers into space. **Children should be supervised here, as a step off the trail could be serious.** The higher one climbs, the greater the views. At 1½ miles the switchbacks end on the crest of the summit ridge. The trail ascends another ½ mile along the sidehill to new views and a final rocky climb to the old lookout site. Even on a foggy day there are flowery rewards; on a clear day, expect magnificence.

Rocky crest of Sauk Mountain

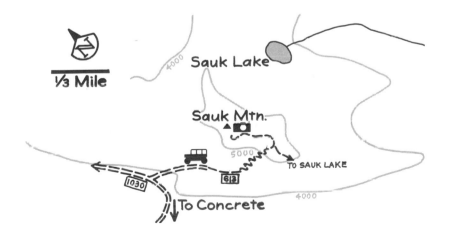

Cascade Pass trail and Eldorado Peak

10. Cascade Pass

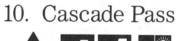

Type	: Dayhike
Difficulty	: Moderate–difficult for children
Hikable	: Mid-July–October
One way	: 4 miles
High point	: 5392 feet
Elevation gain	: 1800 feet
Green Trails map	: No. 80 Cascade Pass
U.S. Forest Service map	: North Cascades Park

The superb meadows and glaciered peaks of Cascade Pass are better than the best of the European Alps. The trail is graded gently enough for children, although the switchbacks gain elevation in maddeningly small increments. At the pass, in season, are myriads of flower species and gasp-provoking views. Or hike it in late fall to admire the color of the vine maple and huckleberry leaves, and a dusting of powdered-sugar snow on the summits.

Drive North Cascade Highway 20 to Marblemount. Instead of turn-

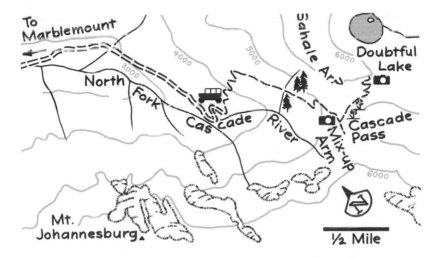

ing left, with the main highway, continue straight, taking the Cascade River road across the Skagit River. Drive about 25 miles to a large parking lot at the road end, elevation 3600 feet.

The trailhead starts switchbacking immediately. At the outset only the bottom cliffs of Mount Johannesburg are visible, but after a mile you can see the mountain's snowfields and hanging glaciers, which almost every summer day send avalanches thundering down. Some children find the sight and sound exciting; others may need reassurance. Still visible nearby are the waste rock and debris from a mine, which from the 1890s to the 1970s extracted no ore of value, but a good deal of money from stock speculators and in the end a large purchase payment from the National Park Service. At about 3 miles the trail gradually emerges from the last patches of forest and at 4 miles tops out at Cascade Pass, 5392 feet.

The pass has had such heavy use that erosion has left the bench-mark 2 feet above the ground surface! No camping is permitted, to allow fragile meadows to recover. You can rest on logs that have been arranged so that one may stare east down the Stehekin Valley or turn around to face the Inspiration Glacier on Eldorado Peak. Flowers climb the slopes in every direction. Clumps of subalpine fir and mountain hemlock beside the scree slopes or next to snow and rock outcrops are the only trees at this altitude, but below are deep green forests rolling out like magic carpets. A park ranger is frequently stationed at the pass and will identify Eldorado, Forbidden, and other peaks. Well-worn trails, excellent for older children, lead up in either of two directions: south to Mix-Up Arm and north up Sahale Arm, from which the trail dips abruptly to the deep cirque of Doubtful Lake.

11. Lake Ann

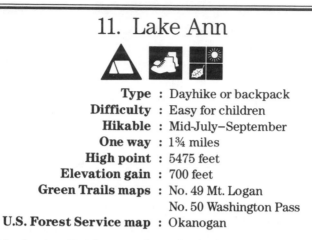

Type :	Dayhike or backpack
Difficulty :	Easy for children
Hikable :	Mid-July–September
One way :	1¾ miles
High point :	5475 feet
Elevation gain :	700 feet
Green Trails maps :	No. 49 Mt. Logan
	No. 50 Washington Pass
U.S. Forest Service map :	Okanogan

This short walk takes you from the highway to the high country, complete with alpine scenery. The lake might even hold a few floating icebergs!

Drive North Cascade Highway 20 east to Rainy Pass and park at the south side rest area, elevation 4800 feet. Find the trail marked "Lakes Trails"; 10 feet along it is the one marked "Lake Ann-Maple Pass."

The hiker-only trail starts on a gentle grade through a rockslide for a scant 1 mile. At 1¼ miles is a junction; go left on the lower trail. The way narrows with roots, rocks, and marshy areas that may impede small feet, but may allow their owners to inspect frogs at close range. At 1¾ miles the trail comes to Lake Ann, elevation 5475 feet.

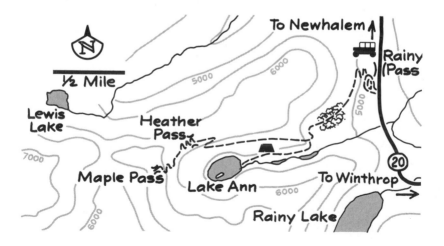

Small children can wade in the outlet stream, ponds, and in the marsh below the lake. Even if the lake has icebergs, the possibilities for stick and stone throwing are infinite, and there's ample room to play.

Camping is not allowed near the lake, but the sites ¼ mile back are good.

Small pond by trail to Lake Ann

12. Heather Pass

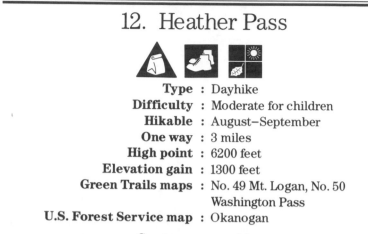

Type	:	Dayhike
Difficulty	:	Moderate for children
Hikable	:	August–September
One way	:	3 miles
High point	:	6200 feet
Elevation gain	:	1300 feet
Green Trails maps	:	No. 49 Mt. Logan, No. 50 Washington Pass
U.S. Forest Service map	:	Okanogan

See map on page 40

So the children had a great time at Lake Ann (Hike 11)? Then they'll surely want to return and continue upward on the same trail to look down on the large iceberg-filled alpine lake. Watch for pikas (conies) scampering the rockslides, and listen for marmots whistling in the meadows. My children used to try to start a dialogue by whistling back.

Follow the directions in Hike 11 and take the Lake Ann trail. At 1¼ miles is a junction. The lower, left fork drops to Lake Ann (Hike 11). Keep right, and climb 1½ miles through penstemon-filled rockeries to Heather Pass, elevation 6200 feet.

Left: Pika. Right: Marmot feeding in alpine meadow

Black Peak, from Heather Pass

The meadow gardens are superb and so are the views: Black Peak above azure Wing Lake, Lewis and Cortco peaks, all framed by alpine larch and mountain hemlock.

Somewhat more steeply, the trail continues 1 mile to 6600-foot Maple Pass, passing over one steep snow slope without a runout, that in most years doesn't melt until mid-August. Try these meadows in September, when the bugs have quit for the season and the berry crop comes in. In all seasons the views from the pass are breathtaking in their scope and alpine grandeur.

Great Horned Owl

North Cascade Highway: East

State Route 20

13. Blue Lake...46
14. Goat Peak...48
15. Ninety-nine Ridge...50
16. Benson Pass...52
17. Black Lake...54

13. Blue Lake

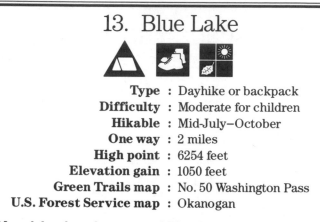

Type :	Dayhike or backpack
Difficulty :	Moderate for children
Hikable :	Mid-July–October
One way :	2 miles
High point :	6254 feet
Elevation gain :	1050 feet
Green Trails map :	No. 50 Washington Pass
U.S. Forest Service map :	Okanogan

Many lakes have been named Blue, but to date this is the only one reached by a designated National Recreation Trail, a formal recognition of its outstanding beauty that does not, unfortunately, preserve it from logging or motorcycles. An abandoned old miner's cabin at the lake makes a good playhouse, and campsites are plentiful near the shoreline.

Drive the North Cascade Highway 20 1 mile west of Washington Pass to the Blue Lake trailhead No. 314, elevation 5200 feet.

Before leaving the car gaze up at Liberty Bell Mountain. Its bell shape seems to change as the trail ascends and becomes more like a turreted castle. Climbers headed to Early Winters Spire share this trail before turning left for their high camp in meadows below the cliffs.

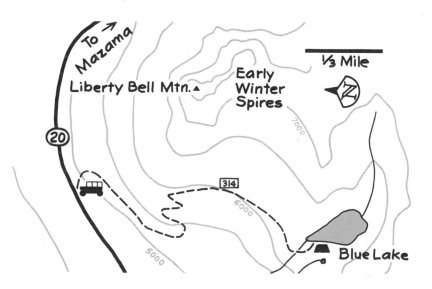

Blue Lake

Trail No. 314 is in good shape and modestly steep. At first highway sounds follow hikers, but at ½ mile they fade out as the path switchbacks from forest to flower-covered avalanche slope. The mix of trees shifts to subalpine firs and larches and heather begins to appear. At 2 miles the outlet stream is crossed; a few feet farther, at 6254 feet, beautiful Blue Lake appears.

The lake is set in a deep cirque below rugged cliffs. For most of the summer the water is kept ice cold by snow fingers beside a rockslide at the far end. Good campsites lie on both sides of the outlet stream. The old miner's cabin should not be relied upon except in direst weather.

Lookout on Goat Peak with Silver Star Mountain in distance

14. Goat Peak

Type : Dayhike
Difficulty : Difficult for children
Hikable : July–October
One way : 2 miles
High point : 7000 feet
Elevation gain : 1400 feet
Green Trails map : No. 51 Mazama
U.S. Forest Service map : Okanogan

A lookout that is still occupied (in fire season) is excitement enough to make this steep and rocky trail seem less steep and rocky. From the North Cascade Highway near Early Winters, you can point it out to the children — a tiny tower perched atop the Goat Wall at the highest point on the northern horizon. Once there, they can peer down to the highway where the cars look like brightly colored ants running along a black ribbon.

The lookout was originally reached — and supplied — by a much longer trail, but the logging road has shortened the walk and a helicopter does the supplying. The mountain goats for which the peak was named, once so abundant, were slaughtered in the 1920s. However, as hunting regulations have become more sensible, they are reoccupying parts of their old range. Methow Valley folks say they have begun, now and then, to spy goats on Goat Wall.

Drive North Cascade Highway 20 to the Methow Valley. Between Early Winters and Winthrop take the road signed "Mazama." About 4 miles east of Mazama go left on road No. 52 for 3.7 miles, then left on road No. 5225, signed "Goat Peak." At 8.3 miles from the county road, go right on road No. (5225)200 another 3 miles to the trailhead, located in a saddle. Elevation is 5600 feet.

Goat Peak trail No. 457 begins in subalpine fir and lodgepole pine, traversing a rocky ridgetop, then ascending rocky meadows. In about ½ mile it tilts upward and steeply switchbacks to a 6800-foot shoulder with good views. It's another half mile of easy ups and downs along the ridge top, culminating in a final steep climb to the summit and lookout tower, 7000 feet.

The ridge vistas are magnificent, spreading east to farms of the Methow Valley and southwest to Silver Star, Mount Gardner, and Varden Creek, hidden by the jumble of mountains around Golden Horn. Children will enjoy talking with the lookout about how to spot fires. The lookout will be glad to have company: he or she doesn't see many fresh faces.

15. Ninety-nine Ridge

Type	:	Dayhike or backpack
Difficulty	:	Moderate for children
Hikable	:	Mid-July–October
One way	:	2 miles
High point	:	7000 feet
Elevation gain	:	600 feet
Green Trails map	:	No. 50 Washington Pass
U.S. Forest Service map	:	Okanogan

This sky-high ridge in the North Cascades above the upper Methow Valley offers spectacular views of Mount Ballard, Azurite Peak, and a maze of mountains to the north, south, east,and west. You will feel like you're halfway to heaven, maybe because you're starting at 6400 feet — the highest starting point in the state — maybe because of the contrast between the rugged mountains and the fragile flowers so abundant here. You feel overwhelmed and at home at the same time.

Drive North Cascade Highway 20 to the Methow Valley. Near Early Winters follow signs to Mazama. Turn upriver at Mazama and go 20 miles on the Methow River road to Harts Pass, elevation 6198 feet. Near the pass turn left and follow Meadow Campground road 2.5 miles to the road end and the Pacific Crest trailhead, elevation 6400 feet.

The trail begins by contouring a steep sidehill, crossing a rockslide high above the site of the (defunct) Brown Bear Mining Camp, and in a long 1/2 mile rounding the shoulder of a ridge into magnificent new views.

Now the slope steepens and the trail narrows. The hillside is a rock garden blooming in Indian paintbrush, lupine, alpine fireweed, and pink Columbia Lewisia that call for close-ups. At 2 miles the trail attains and catwalks a 7000-foot ridge crest between Ninety-nine Basin and Trout Creek. For dayhikers this is a good stopping point, with views north along the Cascade Crest and to the glaciers on Mount Ballard and Azurite Peak, and the Pacific Crest Trail slanting up meadows to Grasshopper Pass. You can also see an abandoned lookout on Slate Peak.

Overnighters go another ½ mile to 6900-foot Tatie Pass. Views here are into the headwaters of Slate Creek. Campsites with water (in early summer) lie several hundred feet down the south side.

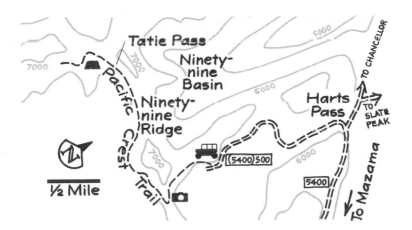

Tatie Pass
Ninety-nine Basin
Pacific Crest Trail
Ninety-nine Ridge
Harts Pass
7000
7000
7000
6000
6000
6000
5000
5400 500
5400
TO CHANCELLOR
TO SLATE PEAK
To Mazama
½ Mile

Pacific Crest Trail on Ninety-nine Ridge

16. Benson Pass

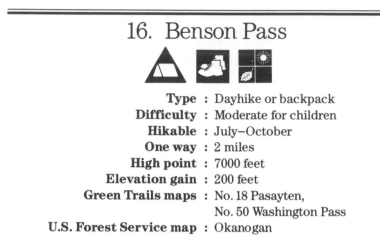

Type	:	Dayhike or backpack
Difficulty	:	Moderate for children
Hikable	:	July–October
One way	:	2 miles
High point	:	7000 feet
Elevation gain	:	200 feet
Green Trails maps	:	No. 18 Pasayten,
		No. 50 Washington Pass
U.S. Forest Service map	:	Okanogan

Pacific Crest Trail traversing toward Benson Pass

A minimum effort yields some of the most gorgeous views and flower-covered meadows in the state. The hike on the Pacific Crest Trail from Harts Pass is gentle enough for a four-year-old, yet awe-inspiring for hikers of all ages. But be prepared for a shock. Across the valley bulldozer tracks zigzag through beautiful alpine meadows, the work of a modern prospector operating under laws passed 120 years ago, not yet amended to fit the 20th century.

Following the directions given in Hike 15, drive to Harts Pass on the Methow River road. Turn right on the Slate Peak road, pass the special trailhead for horses, and at 1.5 miles, at an abrupt switchback, find a small pull-off parking area and the trailhead, elevation 6800 feet.

The trail starts with a short climb into a meadow, then levels out and joins the Pacific Crest Trail as it contours under the summit of Slate Peak and its old lookout tower. Look out to Silver Star, the Mount Gardner massif, Azurite Peak, and Colonial in the distance. Watch or hold chil- dren to make sure they don't stumble — the slope on the left, the view side, drops thousands of feet to Slate Creek. The flowers here are the envy of gardeners for their diversity and constant bloom throughout the summer season. In August expect bluebells, shrubby cinquefoil, stonecrop, lupine, and Indian paintbrush.

At 1¾ miles the trail contours above Benson Basin and at 2 miles reaches Benson Pass, elevation 6700 feet, with views down the West Fork of the Pasayten River. There are two small campsites here, with water several hundred feet back along the trail. For better camping drop 250 feet into Benson Basin. Practice no-trace camping here, using a stove instead of a fire — the small subalpine firs and larches at 6500 feet took a long time to grow. Windy Pass is 2 miles farther, offering different panoramas and more beauty-spot gardens — but then, so does the entire route to the Canadian Border. The kids will dream of the time they can hike *there.*

17. Black Lake

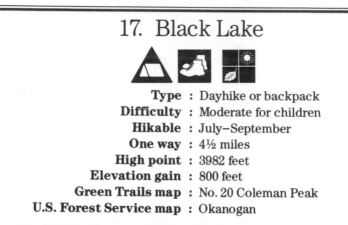

Type	: Dayhike or backpack
Difficulty	: Moderate for children
Hikable	: July–September
One way	: 4½ miles
High point	: 3982 feet
Elevation gain	: 800 feet
Green Trails map	: No. 20 Coleman Peak
U.S. Forest Service map	: Okanogan

Black Lake is one of the gentlest trails for small children in the whole Pasayten Wilderness. Surrounded by forest, the lake is a destination with attractions for everyone — fishing, swimming, wading, birding, and just sitting and looking at mountain scenery.

Drive the Chewack River road north from Winthrop. Upon entering the National Forest the road becomes No. 51 and in a few miles No. 5160. At 20.7 miles from Winthrop, turn left on Lakes Creek road No. (5160)100 and drive 2.4 miles to the road end and trail No. 500, elevation 3162 feet.

The wide, level trail follows Lake Creek through a delightful forest sprinkled with wild raspberries and blueberries that normally ripen in August. At about 1½ miles is a 10-by-20-foot boulder that rolled down from a ridge above in the winter of 1984-85, crashed through trees, bounced, then wedged itself between four trees only a few feet from the trail. Assure the children it is unlikely to move from there.

At a little over 2 miles you enter the Pasayten Wilderness. The trail is

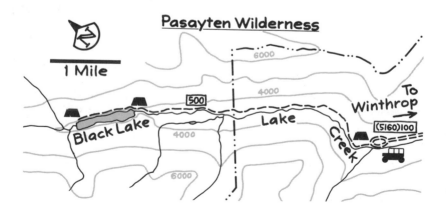

easy the rest of the way, and at 4½ miles reaches the shore of Black Lake, 3982 feet.

Children will want to wade along parts of the mile-long shore. Both ends have clean, spacious campsites, but those at the far end seem to be horse camps. All around the lake are forest-covered ridges, 7000 feet high.

Black Lake

Summer snowbank

Mountain Loop Highway

State Routes 92 and 530

18. Boulder River Waterfall...58
19. Kennedy Hot Springs...60
20. Goat Lake...62
21. Heather Lake...64
22. Lake Twenty-Two...66
23. Boardman Lake...68
24. Ashland Lakes...70
25. Kelcema Lake...72
26. Big Four Ice Caves...74
27. Independence Lake...76
28. Barlow Point Trail...78
29. Monte Cristo Road...80
30. Cutthroat Lakes...82

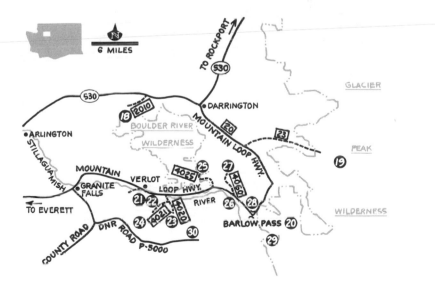

18. Boulder River Waterfall

Type	:	Dayhike or backpack
Difficulty	:	Easy for children
Hikable	:	March–November
One way	:	1¼ miles
High point	:	1200 feet
Elevation gain	:	250 feet
Green Trails maps	:	No. 77 Oso and
		No. 109 Granite Falls
U.S. Forest Service map	:	Mt. Baker–Snoqualmie

A gentle trail, smooth and level enough for small children, takes families comfortably through old-growth forest beside a glacier-fed river in the Boulder River Wilderness. A magnificent destination is the spectacular wall-curtain waterfall at 1¼ miles. A bit beyond, an open area by the river makes a pleasant camp or lunch stop. One particular reason for preserving this valley as wilderness is that it contains one of the few remaining low-elevation old-growth forests. Foresters estimate the age of some of the trees at 750 years. All along the path are awesome old-growth Sitka spruce, silver fir, western red cedar, western hemlock, and Douglas fir. The accompanying mosses, ferns, berries, shrubs, and flowers are samples of what, before logging, all the low-elevation North Cascades valleys were like.

Drive Highway 530 east from Arlington 20 miles toward Darrington; near Milepost 41 turn right on road No. 2010, pass French Creek Campground, and at 3.6 miles from the highway, at a major switchback, find the Boulder Creek trail, elevation 950 feet:

The walk begins on the bed of an old logging railroad — wide, smooth, and well graded. The trail narrows at ½ mile and ambles through big trees shrouded with moss. At 1 mile it passes above Boulder Falls, which lies in a canyon so deep that it can hardly be heard and is impossible to safely view. A short distance beyond, a side trail drops to the river, and several campsites. The river has carved its channel so sharply that there is no flood plain, leaving the trail nowhere to go except on a narrow shelf between cliffs. At 1¼ miles, across the river, is the first of two waterfalls tumbling off cliffs into the river. By midsummer the tumble is a quiet trickle, but thanks to the low elevation hikers can come in early spring, even winter, when higher trails are plugged up with snow.

Unnamed waterfall and Boulder River

Children enjoy hopping about in the spray and mist. This makes a fine lunch stop.

The trail continues another 3 miles to Boulder River Ford and a nice campsite next to the river.

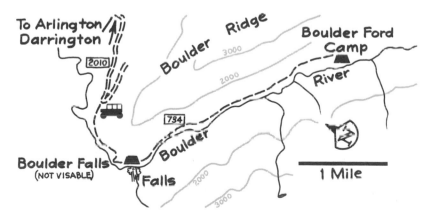

19. Kennedy Hot Springs

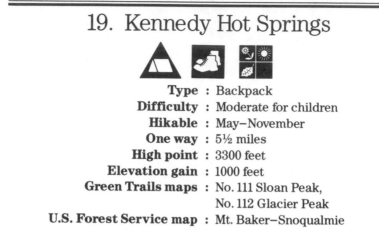

Type :	Backpack
Difficulty :	Moderate for children
Hikable :	May–November
One way :	5½ miles
High point :	3300 feet
Elevation gain :	1000 feet
Green Trails maps :	No. 111 Sloan Peak,
	No. 112 Glacier Peak
U.S. Forest Service map :	Mt. Baker–Snoqualmie

Kennedy Hot Springs

Of the several hot springs in the Cascades, these are particularly popular with hikers and families. The trail is almost level and fairly wide for much of the way. Glorious old-growth trees canopy the way. Soaking in the pool is a little like soaking in a hot tub filled with tepid iron oxide water, but timing is everything. After the 5-mile hike in, the experience is welcome. Because of the distance, plan to camp overnight.

Drive Highway 530 to Darrington. Where the highway makes a sharp left turn upon entering the town, go straight ahead and find the Mountain Loop Highway. In about 3 miles enter the Mount Baker–Snoqualmie National Forest, where the road becomes No. 20. At 10.5 miles cross the Sauk River. Go left on the White Chuck River road No. 23 and drive another 11 miles to the parking area at the road end, elevation 2300 feet.

The wide, gentle forest trail rambles beside the White Chuck River. The word "chuck" is Chinook jargon for "water." The water is white from glacial silt descending from tributaries high on Glacier Peak. At 5¼ miles cross Glacier Creek on a log to campsites near the Kennedy Guard Station; more are located across the river. Elevation, 3200 feet.

Cross the bridge over the White Chuck to see steam rising from the mineralized water in a wooden 5-foot-by-5-foot pool. Unless you are very lucky, you will also see a crowd of other bathers. The purity of the water may be in question after a dozen people have bathed in it, and there is a good chance that some hikers will be bathing in the nude, so parents may wish to arrange to take the trip midweek in April or May. When there are fewer people, it is truly invigorating to alternate dips in the pool and the river, a Finnish sauna experience.

20. Goat Lake

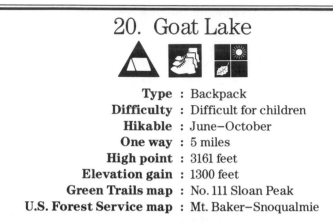

Type : Backpack
Difficulty : Difficult for children
Hikable : June–October
One way : 5 miles
High point : 3161 feet
Elevation gain : 1300 feet
Green Trails map : No. 111 Sloan Peak
U.S. Forest Service map : Mt. Baker–Snoqualmie

This is an alpine lake with a history. At the turn of the century optimistic miners built a town here, expecting to find a lode of silver — or lead at least. Above the lake, on the cliffs of Foggy Peak, you can look for old mine shafts, easily recognized by their waste heaps and the ruins of ore-car rails leading into them. Higher still are glaciers and waterfalls tumbling down the cliffs of Foggy Peak. The trail follows the route of a wagon road used at the time of the Monte Cristo mining boom in the 1890s.

Drive the Mountain Loop Highway east from Darrington or, as described here, east from Granite Falls to the Verlot Public Service Center. From the Center go 19.5 miles to Barlow Pass and continue another 4 miles toward Darrington. About 0.2 mile beyond the Elliott Creek Bridge go right 1 mile on road No. 4080 to a large parking lot and trailhead, elevation 1900 feet.

Old maps show the trail starting at the low end of the parking lot. Unfortunately, this trail is abandoned and not recommended for children. The correct way is on the uphill side of the parking lot following an abandoned road. While road walking is less fun, there are views of Elliott Creek valley, Sheep Mountain, the deep gash of Pearsall Creek, and, downstream, Twin Peaks and Dickerman Mountain. At 3½ miles the road turns into a real trail and enters the Henry Jackson Wilderness. At 4½ miles four steep switchbacks ascend through old second-growth forest. In another ½ mile is the Goat Lake outlet, 3162 feet. Children enjoy playing and wading in this pretty lake, although the glacier-fed water is chilly.

Camping is not permitted on the shore, to allow it to recover from overuse, but picnicking is delightful. Campsites are located at the site of an old hotel on a knoll above the lake. Paying guests appreciated this spot 80 years ago, and today's families can see why.

Goat Lake and Cadet Peak

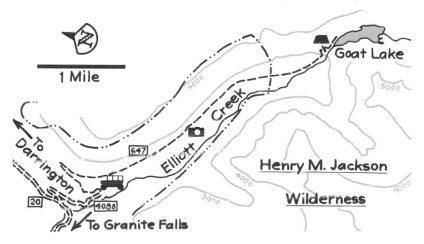

Heather Lake

21. Heather Lake

Type	: Dayhike or backpack
Difficulty	: Moderate for children
Hikable	: Mid-June–October
One way	: 2 miles
High point	: 2400 feet
Elevation gain	: 1000 feet
Green Trails map	: No. 109 Granite Falls
U.S. Forest Service map	: Mt. Baker–Snoqualmie

The steep and rocky trail ascends through magnificent old-growth cedar and hemlock to a lake in a cirque at the foot of Mount Pilchuck. The trail begins on a 1940s logging road, comfortably wide but surfaced with sharp rock. Children will find footing difficult in places and toddlers may need to be carried. The last ½ mile winds through big trees. The lake is large enough for children to wade and splash in.

CAUTION

64

Drive east of Everett on U.S. 2 and follow signs to Stevens Lake. Turn left on State Highway 9, then right on Highway 92 to the town of Granite Falls. Pass through the town and turn left on the Mountain Loop Highway. Follow it to 1 mile east of the Forest Service's Verlot Public Service Center and turn right on Mount Pilchuck road No. 42. Continue 1.5 miles to the Heather Lake trailhead parking lot, elevation 1400 feet.

Trail No. 701 begins 100 yards up the road from the parking area. Two long switchbacks on loose, sharp rock make the first ½ mile tiresome, but at 1 mile the trail leaves the roadbed and the beauty begins. The trail enters old-growth cedars and follows Heather Creek. A waterfall is a good place for a rest stop; large flat rocks are even provided by Mother Nature.

The sounds of Heather Creek call one up to its source. In the next mile six more switchbacks culminate in a puncheon bridge where the trail levels out. Begin a slight descent through open forest to a meadowy basin under the walls of Mount Pilchuck and the lake, elevation 2400 feet.

Campsites are few, and the Forest Service permits none within 100 feet of the shore in order to let some of the mud start growing flowers again. Swimming on the south shore of the lake is a surefire delight for children. The lake is so popular that all camps are filled early on weekends; a better plan is to come on a weekday.

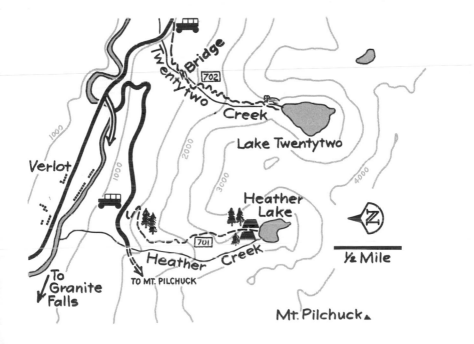

22. Lake Twenty-two

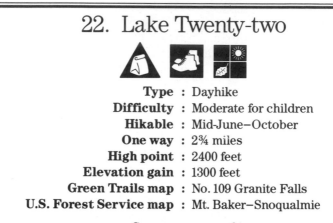

Type	: Dayhike
Difficulty	: Moderate for children
Hikable	: Mid-June–October
One way	: 2¾ miles
High point	: 2400 feet
Elevation gain	: 1300 feet
Green Trails map	: No. 109 Granite Falls
U.S. Forest Service map	: Mt. Baker–Snoqualmie

See map on page 64

The most popular trail in the Stillaguamish valley climbs through ancient cedar trees, past picture-perfect waterfalls, up an old rockslide overgrown with bright vine maple, to a cliff-bordered subalpine lake. The lake's elevation is low enough to take children there quite early in summer or late October. The trail has some steep places but is generally gradual and well maintained.

Drive the Mountain Loop Highway east from Granite Falls to the Forest Service's Verlot Public Service Center (Hike 21). Continue east on the Mountain Loop Highway for 2 miles to a parking area on the right side, approximately 0.25 mile past the Twenty-two Creek highway bridge, elevation 1100 feet.

The wide trail immediately plunges into deep shade, contouring the hillside to Twenty-two Creek, and crossing it on a "Billy Goat Gruff" bridge in ⅓ mile. Small children love looking down from the bridge to the white tumult of waterfalls.

Beyond the bridge the trail begins a series of switchbacks, climbing steadily through old-growth forest, crossing a talus slope, and going near several exciting waterfalls. At 2¾ miles is the outlet of Lake Twenty-two, elevation 2400 feet.

One year, on the Fourth of July, we found it still snowed in, but that was an unusual year. Usually the only permanent snowfield is at the lake's opposite end. No camping is permitted.

Lake Twenty-two trail

23. Boardman Lake

Type :	Dayhike or backpack
Difficulty :	Easy for children
Hikable :	Mid-June–October
One way :	¾ mile
High point :	2981 feet
Elevation gain :	200 feet
Green Trails map :	No. 110 Silverton
U.S. Forest Service map :	Mt. Baker–Snoqualmie

Two large forest lakes lie within ¾ mile of the car. The first, Lake Evan, is just off the road — convenient for parents of toddlers who seek a wooded picnic spot. The second, Boardman Lake, with only 200 feet of trail elevation to gain, is deeper, cleaner and larger, and offers trout fishing and views of Bald Mountain. Children will enjoy wading and splashing from the shore, whether the stay is for a day or overnight.

Drive the Mountain Loop Highway 4.5 miles east from the Forest Service's Verlot Public Service Center (Hike 21), turn right on Schweitzer Creek road No. 4020, and continue for 5 miles, passing junctions with roads No. 4021 and No. 4024, to the trailhead, elevation 2800 feet.

Trail No. 704 is smooth and well maintained; the path, surfaced with crushed gravel, travels through gardenlike old-growth forest whose immense cedars are often topless. These patriarchs are many centuries in growing to such size, and centuries in the dying, bit by bit. Lake Evan

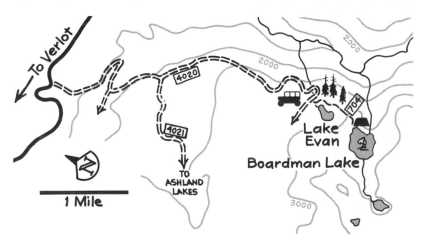

Boardman Lake

has one marshy campsite and a backcountry toilet. Boardman Lake, elevation 2981 feet, offers five sites plus a group camp, each equipped with benches and fire pits. In midsummer children can feast on the delicious ripe huckleberries that flourish along the shore.

Beaver Plant Lake

24. Ashland Lakes

Type	:	Dayhike or backpack
Difficulty	:	Moderate for children
Hikable	:	July–October
One way	:	1¾ miles
High point	:	3000 feet
Elevation gain	:	500 feet
Green Trails map	:	No. 110 Silverton
U.S. Forest Service map	:	Mt. Baker–Snoqualmie

A chain of three pretty woodland lakes located on Department of Natural Resources land is at the end of a rough, marshy trail. Child-delighting boardwalks encircle all of Upper Ashland and parts of Beaver Plant and Lower Ashland lakes. Campsites are at all three lakes.

Drive the Mountain Loop Highway east 4.5 miles beyond the Forest

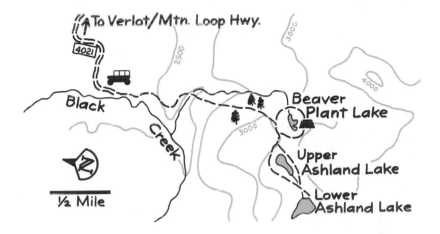

Service's Verlot Public Service Center (Hike 21) and turn right on Schweitzer Creek road No. 4020. At 2.3 miles from the highway turn right onto Bear Lake road No. 4021. Follow this road for another 1.5 miles to the junction with the Bald Mountain–Ashland Lakes road No. (4021)016. Turn left and follow this road 0.2 mile to the trailhead, elevation 2500 feet. Perhaps to discourage jeep and snowmobile traffic, the DNR has removed a bridge, replacing it with a log, and put in deep tank traps along the last 0.6 mile of this road. Stop and walk where it becomes necessary.

This trail has some root outcroppings larger than small children and is scored with deep cuts. Keep going — beautiful old-growth forest begins after ¾ mile, and it is only ¼ mile more under a canopy of giant old cedars and hemlocks to Beaver Plant Lake, where there are developed campsites but no beavers. The lake is shallow, warm, and has a soft mud bottom.

Continue ½ mile on a swampy trail over alternating boardwalk and log ends to Upper Ashland Lake, elevation 300 feet. The lake is lined with reeds, pink swamp laurel, marsh marigolds, and water lilies. You will also find rest rooms, a group camp circle at one end, and two fishing piers with benches. Wooden boardwalks will tempt most children to run and stamp their way around the small lake. In summer the lake becomes warm enough for children to paddle, but because of its muddy bottom, they should be carefully supervised. Huckleberries in season are delicious.

For a different type of lake, drop 300 feet in ¼ mile to Lower Ashland Lake. This section of trail has enough roots that toddlers will have trouble, but the deep clear lake is reason to carry them for this short distance.

Kelcema Lake

25. Kelcema Lake

Type	:	Dayhike or backpack
Difficulty	:	Easy for children
Hikable	:	June–October
One way	:	½ mile
High point	:	3142 feet
Elevation gain	:	80 feet
Green Trails map	:	No. 110 Silverton
U.S. Forest Service map	:	Mt. Baker–Snoqualmie

This easy walk takes you through subalpine forest to a large cirque lake. Small children can happily throw stones and sticks in the water for hours, or jump in for other water games. This site was once a Boy Scout camp, attained only by a trail that started way down in the valley bottom and climbed all the way in virgin forest.

Drive the Mountain Loop Highway 14.5 miles east from the Forest Service's Verlot Public Service Center (Hike 21). Turn left on Deer Creek road No. 4052, and continue for 4.5 miles, at one point fording a stream (on a concrete base) to the trailhead, elevation 3100 feet.

Park and find trail No. 718, starting in a small marshy meadow. (In June you can see bog orchids, marsh marigolds, grass of parnassus, and chocolate bells here.) The trail enters the Boulder River Wilderness, and penetrates an old forest cresting a small knoll that overlooks the lake outfall. Part of the trail is over glacier-carved bedrock, exposed by trail builders for the width of the trail. In ½ mile is the lake, elevation 3142 feet. Some 1600 feet above looms Bald Mountain (a different Bald Mountain than the one seen from Boardman Lake [Hike 23]).

Large campsites lie amid rock buttresses. The water, dark and deep, appears to have fish. On the north side of the lake are old and splendid Alaska cedars, many more campsites, and a backcountry toilet.

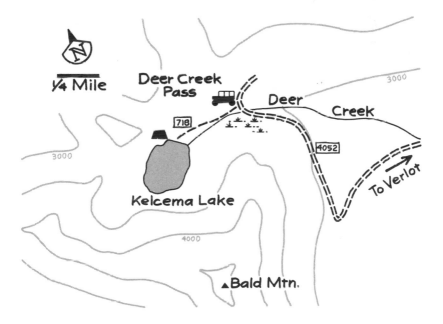

26. Big Four Ice Caves

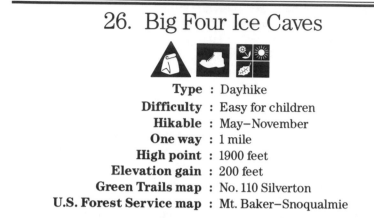

Type : Dayhike
Difficulty : Easy for children
Hikable : May–November
One way : 1 mile
High point : 1900 feet
Elevation gain : 200 feet
Green Trails map : No. 110 Silverton
U.S. Forest Service map : Mt. Baker–Snoqualmie

The nearly level trail, smooth and well maintained, crosses a series of water-spanning bridges and marsh-spanning planked walkways before arriving at the ice caves in the snowfields at the base of the 4000-foot north face of Big Four Mountain. Hike to a stopping point beneath the tall, wide cirque headwall, dappled with snowpatches and waterfalls. The ice caves are formed when the undersides of avalanche snowbanks melt from the action of water and wind. They vary in size and shape from year to year. They do not open until midsummer and are never safe to enter — ceilings have been known to collapse.

Drive the Mountain Loop Highway 15 miles east from the Forest Service's Verlot Public Service Center (Hike 21) to the Big Four parking area, elevation 1700 feet. The old chimney is all that remains of an inn that stood here from 1922 until it burned to the ground in 1949.

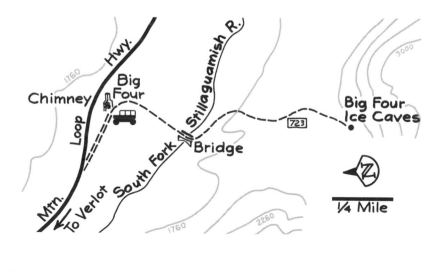

Big Four Ice Caves

Find the plank trail crossing the marsh (it used to be a golf course!) and swamp. Older kids will have fun stamping along the planks and bridges. Hold tight to the hands of toddlers here. The marsh is punctuated with bright yellow skunk cabbage, marsh marigolds, and such birds as kingfishers, nuthatches, and hairy woodpeckers. The gnawed branches and trees are signs that beavers are at work.

Cross the South Fork of the Stillaguamish at ½ mile and Ice Creek immediately afterward. Two benches offer welcome sitdowns for parents packing babies. A gentle uphill through forest leads to the big picture of Big Four Mountain. The caves can be seen at the foot of a snowfield fan. If you examine the great cliff, you can spot avalanche chutes down which the snow slides in winter and the water falls year-round. If it's a hot day, cool off near the refrigerated caves and enjoy their unusual shapes and pale blue tones.

27. Independence Lake

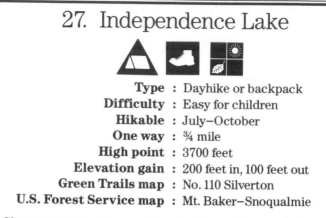

Type :	Dayhike or backpack
Difficulty :	Easy for children
Hikable :	July–October
One way :	¾ mile
High point :	3700 feet
Elevation gain :	200 feet in, 100 feet out
Green Trails map :	No. 110 Silverton
U.S. Forest Service map :	Mt. Baker–Snoqualmie

Close enough to the road for families with small children, small enough to retain warmth from the summer sun, and large enough for

Independence Lake

several campsites, Independence Lake was named for a nearby 19th-century mining claim. One August my delighted children swam all afternoon, disappointed only that we had not brought camping gear so that we might have stayed overnight.

Drive the Mountain Loop Highway 15 miles past the Verlot Public Service Center (Hike 21) and turn right on Coal Lake road No. 4060. (Children — and drivers — may consider this a scary road because it is steep, narrow, and has a sharp drop-off on one side, but the views of Big Four Mountain are spectacular.) Drive 4.8 miles, passing Coal Lake, to the end of the road, elevation 3600 feet.

Trail No. 712 is a little hard to find. Look for it on the upper hillside of the parking lot. After zigzagging a few hundred yards, it enters old- growth forest and descends ¼ mile, then climbs gradually for the remaining ½ mile. Roots and rocks in the trail may trip up very young children, but the distance is so short they can be carried. Watch for lily of the valley and salmonberries. The trail climbs again, gradually, to reach the lake, a very deep one set beneath rock cliffs 1000 feet tall. Independence Lake, elevation 3700 feet, is popular with fishermen (who might object to the splashing and diving of kids). My children thought the northwest end was sunnier and best for swimming.

At least six campsites can be found if you decide to overnight here. North Lake Pass would make a fine additional dayhike — views are excellent at North Lake, 2½ miles farther along the trail.

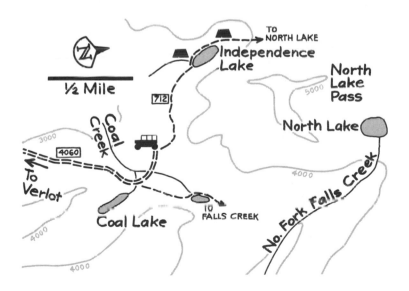

28. Barlow Point Trail

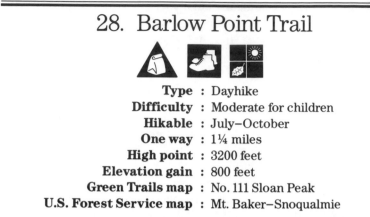

Type	:	Dayhike
Difficulty	:	Moderate for children
Hikable	:	July–October
One way	:	1¼ miles
High point	:	3200 feet
Elevation gain	:	800 feet
Green Trails map	:	No. 111 Sloan Peak
U.S. Forest Service map	:	Mt. Baker–Snoqualmie

Steep switchbacks lead to a sweeping viewpoint of the south forks of the Sauk and Stillaguamish rivers, but this trail is short and to the point! Older children will feel a sense of accomplishment at climbing 800 feet in 1¼ miles and parents will enjoy the views from the rocky summit.

Drive the Mountain Loop Highway to the Forest Service's Verlot Public Service Center (Hike 21), then continue east 19.4 miles toward

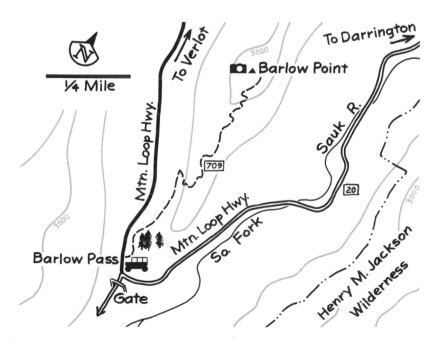

Valley of the South Fork Sauk River, from Barlow Point

Barlow Pass. Just short of the pass, on the left side of the road, is a short spur to the parking lot, elevation 2400 feet. (If the lot is full, park beside the highway.) The unsigned Barlow Point trail No. 709 is on the west side of the parking lot.

The way begins in shady forest. At ⅓ mile you cross the original Government Trail, then the grade of the Everett and Monte Cristo Railroad. Keep right on the trail, which begins switchbacking at the foot of a large basalt rock outcrop. I counted 26 short switchbacks climbing to Barlow Point, which is at the end of a long ridge, 3200 feet. At the top, imagine being in the old lookout tower that once stood here, and scan the hillsides and peaks for lightning strikes or smouldering campfires.

South Fork Sauk River and the Monte Cristo road

29. Monte Cristo Road

Type :	Dayhike or backpack
Difficulty :	Easy for children
Hikable :	May–November
One way :	1 mile, 2½ miles
High point :	2500 feet
Elevation gain :	100 feet
Green Trails maps :	No. 111 Sloan Peak, No. 143 Monte Cristo
U.S. Forest Service map :	Mt. Baker–Snoqualmie

A 1980 flood changed the dusty county road leading to Monte Cristo, a historic mining townsite, into a popular 4-mile trail. The owners of property in the old townsite occasionally "jeep" the road, but it is gated to public vehicles. Children enjoy being able to walk abreast with

parents, pausing along the way to splash in backwater pools of the South
Fork of the Sauk River. There's really no need to hike the whole distance;
though the area reeks of history, fire and snow have left little to see — the
river, forest, and peaks are the best features. Better, instead, to stay or
turn around at one of the spots that used to be crowded car campsites
and are now lightly used hikers' camps.

Drive the Mountain Loop Highway 19.4 miles east of the Forest
Service's Verlot Public Service Center (Hike 21) to the end of the pavement at Barlow Pass, elevation 2400 feet. The graveled Mountain Loop
Highway bends north. A gate marks the road/trail to Monte Cristo; it
begins in alder and maple forest, the river on the left. At 1 mile you'll find
abundant campsites at the Gothic Basin trailhead.

After you cross the river on a makeshift wooden bridge, you'll begin
to see vistas of snowcapped peaks — the Wilman Spires. Continue
upriver; the road is almost level to a second camp at 2½ miles, elevation
2400 feet.

Older kids, those old enough to have an interest in history, may want
to go on from the second campsite another 1½ miles to the site of the
1890s mining town. Unfortunately, most of the history has vanished
under winter avalanches and green growth, and the town's few remaining
cabins are privately owned, but the old railroad turntable on the right, a
powerhouse, and the Monte Cristo town map posted on a wooden sign let
the imagination visualize the days when the Rockefellers, Colbys, and
Hoyts invested hundreds of thousands of dollars in mining equipment
and the Everett and Monte Cristo Railroad, betting on a bonanza. Though
gold, silver, lead, and nickel were found, the river kept wiping out the
railroads, the Mother Lode never revealed itself, and the bubble burst in
1899, when Rockefeller financing pulled out.

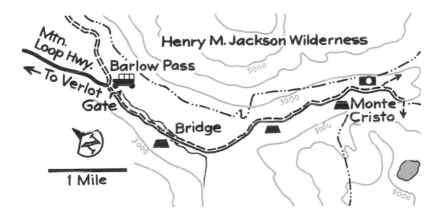

One of the five Cutthroat Lakes

30. Cutthroat Lakes

Type	:	Dayhike or backpack
Difficulty	:	Difficult for children
Hikable	:	July–October
One way	:	3½ miles
High point	:	4500 feet
Elevation gain	:	1500 feet in, 400 feet out
Green Trails maps	:	No. 110 Silverton, No. 142 Index
U.S. Forest Service map	:	Mt. Baker–Snoqualmie

These five exquisite alpine lakes are remote enough to be relatively uncrowded. Families who wish to camp can spend several days sitting and admiring the lakes' contours, or wandering and exploring.

From the Mountain Loop Highway at the east end of Granite Falls turn right on South Alder. At 0.3 mile turn left on East Pioneer. At 4.5 miles from this junction look sharp on the left for an insignificant sign marking Department of Natural Resources road No. P-5000. Drive this road 12.4 miles to a junction with an alternative access, from Sultan via Olney Pass. Continue on No. P-5000 and at about 20 miles from Granite Falls cross Williamson Creek on a concrete bridge and follow it upstream. In 1.6 miles from the bridge, go straight ahead at a junction. Slightly past the junction, turn left and cross Williamson Creek, watching for signs for the Bald Mountain trail. The road switchbacks upward through DNR clearcuts around and above Spada Lake and the Everett watershed. About 4 miles after crossing Williamson Creek, you reach the Bald Mountain trailhead, elevation 3000 feet. The maps for this hike overlap at the critical point between access roads and the lakes, and for that reason are confusing and difficult to use.

The trail begins on a washed-out jeep road through a clearcut. Keep right at the first of two side roads and left at the second. The road/trail climbs steadily and contours around a hill with spectacular views the length of Spada Lake reservoir and beyond to Vesper and Del Campo peaks. At 1 mile the road yields to true trail, which enters trees and winds upward. At least two scramble pitches are not hazardous, but require using hands; children may need help. At 2 miles cross a large rockslide, at 2¼ miles emerge into the first of the steep alpine meadows, and at 2½ miles you attain the high point, elevation 4500 feet.

Berries and heather cover the slopes. In a few hundred feet the Bald Mountain summit trail goes left. You continue straight ahead, dropping almost 1 mile on a winding trail under Bald Mountain to the largest lake, elevation 4100 feet. It features a rocky island, and coves and inlets to tempt swimmers and campers.

One must explore a bit to find all the lakes and ponds. The terrain is heather-covered hummocks, big subalpine trees, large white granodiorite boulders, and grassy meadows. No child will ever want to leave.

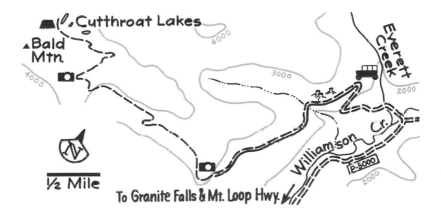

Zephyr Anglewing butterfly in alpine meadow

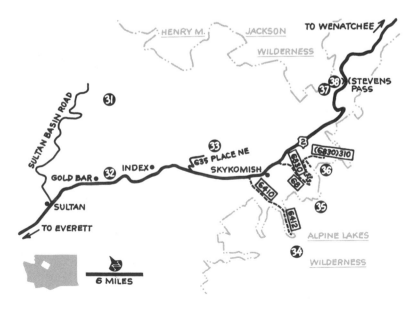

Stevens Pass Highway: West

U.S. 2

31. Boulder Lake...86

32. Wallace Falls...88

33. Barclay Lake...90

34. Lake Dorothy...92

35. Trout Lake...94

36. Tonga Ridge...96

37. Stevens Pass Lakes...98

38. Lake Valhalla...100

Oyster mushrooms along a forest trail

31. Boulder Lake

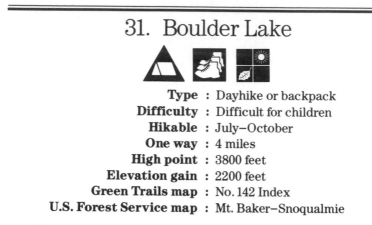

Type :	Dayhike or backpack
Difficulty :	Difficult for children
Hikable :	July–October
One way :	4 miles
High point :	3800 feet
Elevation gain :	2200 feet
Green Trails map :	No. 142 Index
U.S. Forest Service map :	Mt. Baker–Snoqualmie

High, remote, and forested, Boulder Lake can be reached by a steep trail that starts on an old road, travels across a rockslide, and up a cliff-ringed valley. The trail, one of three in the Sultan Basin tree farm, briefly follows Boulder Creek, then rejoins it at its source, the lake. Children will find the lakeshore camps and the smooth swimming beach delightful.

Drive U.S. Highway 2 to Sultan, and at the east edge of town turn left on the Sultan Basin Recreation Area road. At 13 miles you cross Olney Pass, enter the Spada watershed, and register as required. A short distance beyond is a three-way junction. Go straight ahead on the middle road, No. 61, for 7.5 miles. Pass numerous side roads and a boat launch; at 1 mile beyond the Greider Lakes trailhead, you'll find the Boulder Lake trailhead, elevation 1600 feet.

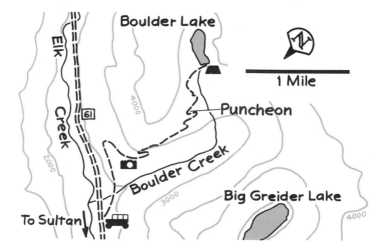

Boulder Lake

The trail begins on an old logging road and in a few hundred yards crosses a wooden bridge over Boulder Creek. (If you hide a watermelon or cold drink in a pool here, it will be icy cold and waiting at the trip's end.) Road grade soon yields to the trail, built by the Department of Natural Resources in 1976. At 1 mile the way crosses a large boulder talus, then climbs through avalanche-slope vine maple and slide alder. At about 1½ miles it switchbacks to climb around a barrier ridge running at right angles across a cliff-walled valley. At 3 miles the way levels out on puncheon to permit easy walking over a marsh. In the forest beyond here, the old firs and cedars are surrounded by moss. Children will be asking, "Are we almost there?" Happily, the answer is "Yes, we are three-fourths of the way." In another mile the trail crosses a bridge over the outlet stream to Boulder Lake, elevation 3800 feet.

The near shore is almost all red and white heather. At the far end are cliffs, ridges, and a rockslide, colorful in fall when set off by the orange of vine maples, but because of the brush and the cliffs you can't get there from here. Six campsites, a good swimming beach, and abundant blueberries and huckleberries in season.

Middle viewpoint of Wallace Falls

32. Wallace Falls

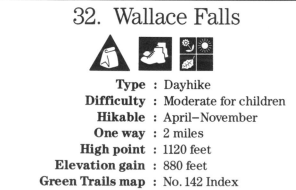

Type : Dayhike
Difficulty : Moderate for children
Hikable : April–November
One way : 2 miles
High point : 1120 feet
Elevation gain : 880 feet
Green Trails map : No. 142 Index
U.S. Forest Service map : None

A spectacular cataract that is visible as far as the Stevens Pass highway, miles away, Wallace Falls in recent years has become easily accessible. The trail is short, sometimes steep, and can be muddy in spring and fall. However, the low elevation means it is open for walking when the highlands are snowed in. Hazards are minimal except at the

trail's end, overlooking the falls, where spray makes every surface slippery and requires every child's hand to be held tight. One Mother's Day I
took two toddlers, a baby, and two mothers to Wallace Falls. The kids had
a grand time (and were carried much of the way), but the mothers never
forgave me!

Drive U.S. 2 east to the town of Gold Bar. Turn left at the sign for
Wallace Falls State Park. Follow more signs to the park headquarters and
trailhead, elevation 300 feet.

The trail starts on a service road under power lines, enters woods,
and in a long ¼ mile forks. The left fork is The Old Railroad Grade Trail,
actually a broad track. The right fork is the Woody Trail, a real trail and
the one I recommend. While the Old Railroad Grade Trail is wide,
smooth, and easy, it takes 2 miles to cover the same distance as the first
mile of the Woody Trail.

The Woody Trail, with many ups and downs, follows near, if not
beside, the Wallace River, often going high above the stream. At 1¼ miles
the trail passes a junction with the Old Railroad Grade Trail, then drops
to a wooden bridge overlooking the North Fork of the Wallace River,
elevation 650 feet. This is a good resting point or a picnic destination if
children are young. The riverbank offers joys that may be sufficiently
satisfying.

But if the roaring of the falls cannot be resisted, climb steeply
onward in old forest. Cross a ridge into the drainage of the South Fork of
the Wallace River and climb to a shelter for the first view.

For even closer views of the thundering cataract continue ½ mile to
the Middle Viewpoint, an ideal place to appreciate the deafening sound
of the huge volume of water.

Finally, ½ mile above the North Fork bridge, the trail ends at Valley
Overlook, elevation 1500 feet.

33. Barclay Lake

Type : Dayhike or backpack
Difficulty : Easy for children
Hikable : June–October
One way : 1½ miles
High point : 2442 feet
Elevation gain : 250 feet
Green Trails map : No. 143 Monte Cristo
U.S. Forest Service map : Mt. Baker–Snoqualmie

This shallow, low-elevation (2442 feet) forest lake lies beneath the massive and spectacular north face of Mount Baring. Children will enjoy the chance to wade, splash, and paddle in this quiet lake, and parents will appreciate the fact that campsites are close enough to the road to make extra trips to the car if necessary. The trail is smooth and gradual, through old-growth forest.

 Drive U.S. 2 east from Everett. About 6 miles east of Index Junction, turn left at Baring on 635th Place Northeast. Cross the railroad track, traverse into the valley of Barclay Creek, and 4.3 miles from the highway reach the trailhead parking area, elevation 2200 feet.

Barclay Lake trail No. 1055 drops from the left side of the road to Barclay Creek and proceeds upstream on an easy, well-maintained trail featuring boardwalks and log ends incised like waffles or manhole covers. Cross the creek on a bridge and watch for a house-size boulder beside the trail; the moss-covered overhang forms a magical cave. I told

Barclay Lake and the shoulder of Mount Baring

my children that elves and dwarves used to live here before America was discovered. It's a short distance from here to the lake.

Campsites extend along the entire north shore of the lake. The Forest Service discourages use of those within 50 feet of the lakeshore; if you decide to stay, try to cooperate.

Gazing up in open-mouthed awe at Mount Baring is enough entertainment for lots of folks. How did such a piece of landscape ever come to be? That's a long and complicated story — mountain building, tectonics plates, etc. But the *steepness* is relatively recent and simple in origin. Of course it's a hard job convincing kids a glacier did this. ("Well, where is it then?" they ask. The answer to this is, "Gone back to Canada for more ice.") For other sport there is a sandy beach for waders and swimmers, and fishing for everyone. Expect weekends to be crowded.

34. Lake Dorothy

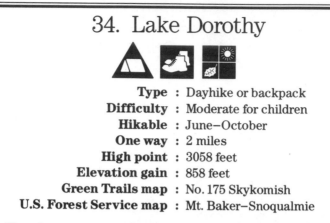

Type	:	Dayhike or backpack
Difficulty	:	Moderate for children
Hikable	:	June–October
One way	:	2 miles
High point	:	3058 feet
Elevation gain	:	858 feet
Green Trails map	:	No. 175 Skykomish
U.S. Forest Service map	:	Mt. Baker–Snoqualmie

The short, very popular, and much-used trail along the rushing Miller River leads quite quickly to one of the largest forest lakes in the Alpine Lakes Wilderness. Opportunities for water activities are abundant. Once the track was so eroded that exposed roots and rocks made travel difficult for short legs. Today, thanks to work by volunteers, the trail is in good shape. Only the last ½ mile is steep, climbing to the source of the Miller, lovely Lake Dorothy.

Drive U.S. 2 east from Everett toward Stevens Pass, and approximately 11 miles east of Index Junction (3.5 miles short of Skykomish, just before the tunnel) go right on the Old Cascade Highway through Money Creek Campground. At 1.2 miles take Miller River road No. 6410, which becomes road No. 6412, and drive to its end.

Camp Robber Creek and the trail to Lake Dorothy

The trail starts in big old cedars and firs. Boggy spots are lighted in spring by torchlike skunk cabbage. At 1¾ miles the trail crosses Camp Robber Creek, on a bridge that is in its own right a sufficient destination. Children can spend a lunch hour stomping back and forth on the bridge to see if their stomps can compete with the waterfall's roar. If they do not recognize John Muir's favorite bird, the water ouzel, tell them to watch for a gray bird skittering along the surface of the water, pausing now and then to perch on a rock, dip-dip-dipping at the knees.

Actually, after Camp Robber Creek the final bit of trail to the lake and its outlet logjam, elevation 3058 feet, are an anticlimax.

The trail continues along the lakeshore to the head, with choice campsites for families arriving early on weekends or midweek. Rocky cliffs rise high on the opposite shore.

Young "hiker" at Trout Lake

35. Trout Lake

Type	:	Dayhike or backpack
Difficulty	:	Easy for children
Hikable	:	June–November
One way	:	1½ miles
High point	:	2150 feet
Elevation gain	:	250 feet
Green Trails map	:	No. 175 Skykomish
U.S. Forest Service map	:	Mt. Baker–Snoqualmie

A gentle trail through magnificent old-growth trees arrives in no time at all at a large forest lake beneath a mountain scarp. Many a tree

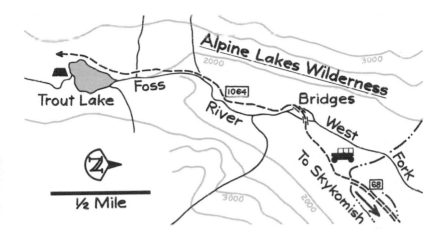

along the way will demand a halt for a stare and questions. And then there's all that water for playing in!

Drive U.S. 2 east from Everett to the town of Skykomish. Continue on U.S. 2 another 1.8 miles and go right on Foss River road No. 68. Follow the river road, passing under a railroad trestle. At 2.5 miles stay right and at 4.8 miles from the highway stay left on road 68 and go 2 miles to the road end and trailhead, elevation 1600 feet.

Trail No. 1064 begins in deciduous bottomland trees — sprawling bigleaf maple and tall cottonwood. Cross the Foss River on a bridge and recross on another. (Children will love this part.) At ½ mile start watching for the big hemlocks and firs, climaxing in the granddaddy of the valley's Douglas firs, some 8 feet in diameter. How old is this patriarch? It sprang from a seed in a fir cone probably about the time Leif Erickson discovered America about a thousand years ago. A large party can try circling the trunk with outstretched arms to get a sense of its girth.

Continue past an enormous boulder at the foot of a rockslide; on a hot day, if you get down on your knees, you can cool your sweaty brow in the chilly air flowing from beneath its edges. The Foss River runs close beside the trail, joined by a succession of tributaries. The stretch of river just before the lake alternates deep pools with rapids and cataracts tumbling over bedrock.

At Trout Lake, 2100 feet, former campsites have been roped off to allow revegetation of overused areas. A posted map shows available campsites at the lake's south end. Fishing here, as the name suggests, plus wading, although the bottom is muddy.

36. Tonga Ridge

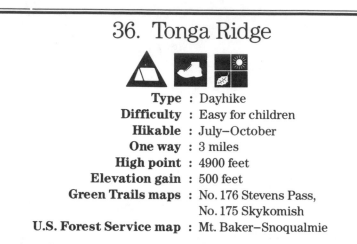

Type	:	Dayhike
Difficulty	:	Easy for children
Hikable	:	July–October
One way	:	3 miles
High point	:	4900 feet
Elevation gain	:	500 feet
Green Trails maps	:	No. 176 Stevens Pass,
		No. 175 Skykomish
U.S. Forest Service map	:	Mt. Baker–Snoqualmie

A trail gradual enough to stroll with small children climbs easily to meadowlands, with views of Glacier Peak and the central Cascades. In fall there are huckleberries to pick; on early summer mornings children can watch for deer.

Drive U.S. 2 east 1.8 miles past Skykomish and go right on Foss River road No. 68. At 2.5 miles turn left on road No. 6830, go another 7 miles, and then turn right on road No. (6830)310. Go 1.5 miles to its end at a parking lot, elevation 4400 feet.

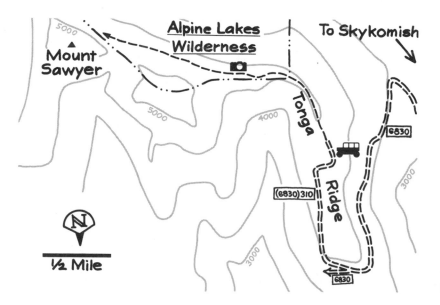

The road ends virtually at timberline, amid spectacular views of Index, Persis, Baring, and Glacier Peak. Why leave the car at all? Because the meadows beckon. Begin on an old fire trail ascending modestly through a forest of mixed conifers. In one mile, the trail breaks out of the forest into broad meadows. The view south to the craggy peaks along the Cascade crest is superb. The trail now follows the crest through meadows of huckleberry and heather.

The views cannot improve — they just change from one gorgeous vista to another. At 3 miles you'll find sometimes watered, sometimes dry campsites at Sawyer Pass, 4800 feet. Try this hike in late September for spectacular fall color and blueberries.

Tonga Ridge trail

37. Stevens Pass Lakes

Type :	Dayhike or backpack
Difficulty :	Moderate for children
Hikable :	July–October
One way :	Skyline Lake: 1½ miles
	Grace Lakes: 1¾ miles
High point :	Skyline Lake: 5092 feet
	Grace Lakes: 4800 feet
Elevation gain :	Skyline Lake: 900 feet
	Grace Lakes: 750 feet
Green Trails maps :	No. 176 Stevens Pass,
	No. 144 Benchmark Mountain
U.S. Forest Service map :	Mt. Baker–Snoqualmie

On each side of Stevens Pass, high above on ridges, are delightful little lakes, Grace Lakes on the south, and Skyline Lake to the north. All are ringed by meadows of heather and blueberries. The lakes are shallow; some may even dry up in late summer, but when full and warm, they make ideal family camps. Unfortunately, to reach any of the lakes requires a hike up steep service roads that can be hot in the noon sun.

Drive U.S. 2 to the summit of Stevens Pass, elevation 4056 feet.

The amazingly remote Skyline Lake is only 1½ miles above the summit. The trail is a steep road suitable for jeeps and 4x4s.

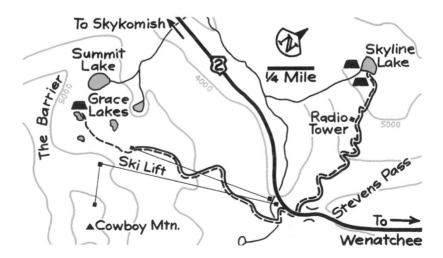

Skyline Lake

Walk or drive ¼ mile up the paved driveway past a number of vacation cabins to a small parking space. Here the road becomes a jeep track and turns uphill with a vengeance — at as much as an 18-percent grade, possible for pedestrians but too rugged for all but a few 4x4s. With every step upward the views of the ski area and surrounding ridges widen. The blueberries here are renowned; commercial pickers spend much of the late summer here, but they don't get 'em all. Here is another source of Energy Food for kids. At 1 mile the trail passes a relay tower in a large clearing and in a steep ½ mile more reaches the lakeshore. Camping here is at the end of the jeep track and across from the outlet. One Labor Day I saw large bear tracks on the shoreline; I hope he enjoyed the juicy blueberries as much as I did.

For Grace Lakes, park on the south side of the pass near the ski area. On the west side of the parking lot find a gated service road. Walk past numerous ski area buildings and with a slight dip, pass directly under chairlifts. Stay left at the first junction and right at the next. Pass under the red chairlift (Barrier Ski Lift) and climb an ever-steepening rocky road to the top terminal of the turquoise Brooks Lift, 4850 feet. Here the road gives way to a boot-beaten path through heather, blueberries, and mountain ash ¼ mile to campsites at the largest of the four shallow, spring-fed Grace Lakes.

For exploration, use the USGS map to reach the other two accessible lakes. The lowest of the Grace Lakes does not have a trail. Summit Lake, the largest and deepest in the Stevens Pass area, is only ¼ mile farther, but it is not recommended for children due to the poor trail.

38. Lake Valhalla

▲	👢	☀🍃

Type	:	Dayhike or backpack
Difficulty	:	Moderate for children
Hikable	:	July–September
One way	:	5½ miles
High point	:	5050 feet
Elevation gain	:	1100 feet in, 200 feet out
Green Trails maps	:	No. 144 Benchmark Mountain,
		No. 176 Stevens Pass
U.S. Forest Service map	:	Wenatchee

Named for the Teutonic home of the gods for good reason — the heather meadows, the rockslides, the ridges and cliffs of Lichtenberg Mountain — Lake Valhalla is the first of a series of lakes north of Stevens Pass on the Pacific Crest Trail. Children will love its fairy-tale charm. Mine told me they thought trolls would live in such a place.

Drive U.S. 2 to the summit of Stevens Pass and park on the north side of the summit area at the east end, elevation 4056 feet. Join the Pacific Crest Trail behind the garage and a power station.

The first 1½ miles, almost level, lie on the original grade of the Great Northern Railroad, constructed over the top of the pass in 1893. The grade was abandoned when the Cascade Tunnel was built in the aftermath of the Wellington Avalanche of 1910, which swept away part of that town and two traincars of people, killing 96. Now it is part of the Pacific Crest Trail.

Along the early part of the hike, look down to the former Yodelin Ski area and cabins, which in 1971 were also struck by a series of avalanches. (The avalanches had been occurring almost every winter, but were never noticed until the developer built in their path.) Views east are down Stevens Creek to Nason Creek and the Stevens Pass Highway. At 1½ miles the trail rounds a ridge, crosses a little stream, and enters Henry M. Jackson Wilderness. The trail is generally well graded and reasonably smooth.

At 2½ miles is a small streamside campsite, and another at 3 miles. At 3½ miles are a meadowy basin and a marsh, where children can pause to do some splashing. Camping is possible here, though not really ideal. A bit farther on, at just under 4 miles, are numerous campsites next to a large meadow. Any one of these campsites would make a good turn-around point for younger children.

The trail climbs to another meadow, elevation 5030 feet, then drops steeply to the shores of Valhalla at 4830 feet, the source of Nason Creek.

Campsites are located at the outlet, with the most numerous and easiest to reach at the upper end. All are popular, so plan to leave home early to get a good spot.

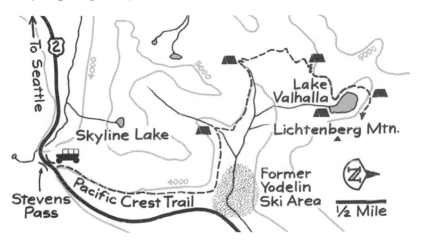

Lake Valhalla

Gray Jay

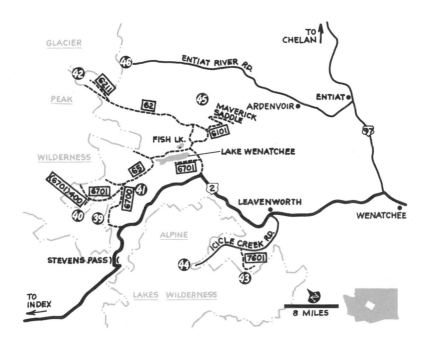

Stevens Pass Highway: East/ Chelan Highway

U.S. 2 and U.S. 97

39. Lake Janus...104

40. Heather Lake...106

41. Hidden Lake...108

42. Spider Meadow...110

43. Eight Mile Lake...112

44. French Creek Campground...114

45. Mad River Vacation...116

46. Myrtle Lake...118

Ptarmigan

39. Lake Janus

Type :	Dayhike or backpack
Difficulty :	Moderate for children
Hikable :	Mid-July–October
One way :	3½ miles
High point :	4680 feet
Elevation gain :	1100 feet in, 700 feet out
Green Trails map :	No. 144 Benchmark Mountain
U.S. Forest Service map :	Wenatchee

The Roman god Janus had two faces, so he could see in two directions at once. A traveler on this trail through the Henry M. Jackson Wilderness can look toward both eastern and western Washington while

Curious deer near Lake Janus

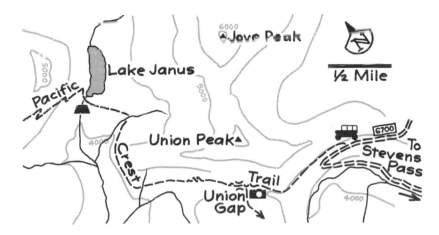

walking the ridge that separates them — the Cascade Crest. Lake Janus, a beauty, is set among alpine meadows at the base of 6007-foot Jove Peak. Adults will enjoy the scenery along the way; children can play in the lake. The trail has some steep portions, but is smooth and well maintained. Note that there is a 700-foot descent; it must be climbed on the return.

Drive U.S. 2, 4.5 miles east from Stevens Pass, and turn left on the Smith Brook road No. 6700. Cross Nason Creek bridge, turn left, and follow the road to the Smith Brook trailhead, elevation 3800 feet. Parking near the trailhead is difficult, so many hikers park 0.25 mile below the last switchback and walk to the trailhead.

Trail No. 1590 switchbacks steeply up to Union Gap, elevation 4680 feet, and a junction with the gentler grade of the Pacific Crest Trail. Views east are toward forests of larch, shimmering aspen, and pines along Nason Creek. The views west are dark with Douglas fir, hemlock, and cedar.

At Union Gap go right, following the Pacific Crest Trail northward, losing 700 feet to pass under cliffs of Union Peak. From this low point the trail climbs again to the shores of Lake Janus, elevation 4146 feet, 3½ miles from the road.

Camping here is good, but crowded by Pacific Crest Trail traffic. The water is clear, deep, and *cold;* children will find it better for skipping stones than for bathing. If you decide to stay, bring a stove — fuel wood is scarce and fires are prohibited.

Heather Lake

40. Heather Lake

Type :	Dayhike or backpack
Difficulty :	Difficult for children
Hikable :	July–October
One way :	3¼ miles
High point :	3953 feet
Elevation gain :	1300 feet
Green Trails map :	No. 144 Benchmark Mountain
U.S. Forest Service map :	Wenatchee

The trail is steep; the lake is big and beautiful. The hot summer day when I was there children were having a fine time swimming and playing on the rocks around the shore.

There are two ways to the Heather Lake trailhead. From Stevens Pass, drive 4.5 miles east, turn left on Smith Brook road No. 6700, and go over Rainy Pass; you continue many more miles over a gravel road to its end at the Heather Lake trailhead. Or, from the north end of Lake Wenatchee go left on the Little Wenatchee River road No. 65, then left on road No. 6700, and cross the Little Wenatchee River to a junction with the Smith Brook road. Go straight ahead on road No. 6701 for 4.7 miles, turn left on road No. (6701)400, and go another 2.3 miles to the road end and trailhead, elevation 2600 feet.

The trail begins in old-growth forest in unprotected Wenatchee National Forest. At 1 mile it crosses Lake Creek and enters the Henry M. Jackson Wilderness. At 1½ miles a series of murderously steep switchbacks climbs 900 feet in a very long mile that will seem like ten. (I went by two boys trying to lug an inflated raft up the trail. I wonder if they made it — the last I saw of them they were complaining that there was no place to set it down.) The grade finally eases and continues another ¾ mile to sparkling Heather Lake, elevation 3953 feet, in a glacier-scooped cirque basin beneath Grizzly Peak. Many good campsites are scattered about among berry bushes and driftwood. Each comes with a view.

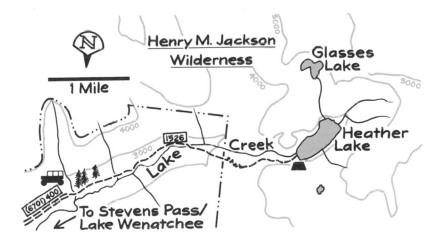

41. Hidden Lake

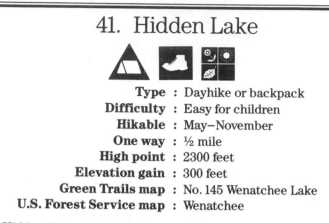

Type	: Dayhike or backpack
Difficulty	: Easy for children
Hikable	: May–November
One way	: ½ mile
High point	: 2300 feet
Elevation gain	: 300 feet
Green Trails map	: No. 145 Wenatchee Lake
U.S. Forest Service map	: Wenatchee

Hidden Lake lies unseen scarcely a half mile above huge Lake Wenatchee. Many families will prefer Hidden Lake, away from the crowds at Lake Wenatchee State Park, for its ponderosa-pine setting and that special feeling only a mountain lake that is located away from a road can provide. One sunny afternoon I watched many parents with toddlers and babies playing at the water's edge.

From U.S. 2 between Stevens Pass and Leavenworth, turn north on Highway 207 toward Lake Wenatchee. At 4 miles turn left to Lake Wenatchee State Park. In a short distance (before the park boundary) turn left again on road No. 6607. Drive 5 miles to Glacier View Campground and trailhead, elevation 2000 feet.

So heavily used that its bony rocks and roots are showing, trail No.

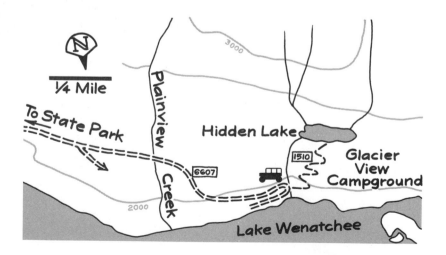

1510 is ¼ mile of steep switchbacks through dry underbrush. Lost on the way is the racket of powerboats on Lake Wenatchee.

Hidden Lake, elevation 2500 feet, is long and narrow, and wraps itself around the base of Nason Ridge. Families, fishermen, and bathers floating in rafts for the joy of floating have a wonderful time in its cool waters.

Hidden Lake

42. Spider Meadow

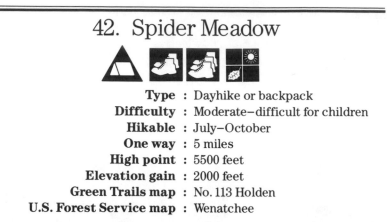

Type	: Dayhike or backpack
Difficulty	: Moderate–difficult for children
Hikable	: July–October
One way	: 5 miles
High point	: 5500 feet
Elevation gain	: 2000 feet
Green Trails map	: No. 113 Holden
U.S. Forest Service map	: Wenatchee

Beneath a spectacular headwall of cliffs and waterfalls sprawls a marvelous wide meadow valley, the reward for a five-mile walk into the Glacier Peak Wilderness. Camping is amid flower fields, beside a cold meandering stream. The deer here are almost tame.

Drive U.S. 2 east 17 miles from Stevens Pass and turn north on the Lake Wenatchee Road. Pass Wenatchee State Park and cross the Wenatchee River. Turn right at the final junction, go 1.5 miles, then turn left on Chiwawa River road No. 62, signed "Trinity." Drive 22 miles, turn right on road No. 6211, signed "Phelps Creek," and go 2 miles to a gate and the trailhead, elevation 3500 feet.

The hike begins on a gated miners' road, passing the Carne Mountain trail at ¼ mile, Box Creek at 1 mile and Chipmunk Creek at 1¾ miles, a good turnaround close to Phelps Creek.

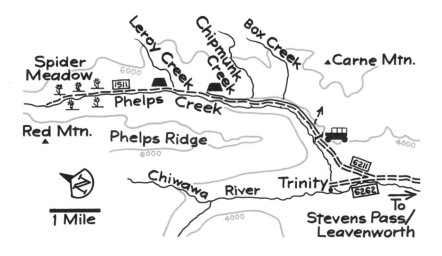

Spider Meadow

At 2⅔ miles, where the road becomes trail, enter the Glacier Peak Wilderness. At 3½ miles cross Leroy Creek and pass the Leroy Creek trail.

All of the creeks are delightful resting places — and campsites, if necessary. From Leroy Creek it's an easy 1½ miles through spruce, noble fir, and alpine flowers or berries in season to Spider Meadow, elevation 5500 feet.

The parkland extends more than a mile north and south, bordered upvalley by the cliffs of Dumbbell and Red mountains. Campsites edge the meadow; walk to the upper end for more secluded campsites at the base of a talus slope, and the ruins of an old miner's cabin. In early morning or evening children may expect to see the curious deer approach camp and play, chasing each other through the flowers.

43. Eightmile Lake

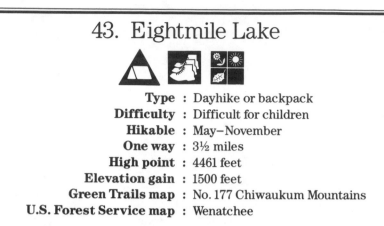

Type :	Dayhike or backpack
Difficulty :	Difficult for children
Hikable :	May–November
One way :	3½ miles
High point :	4461 feet
Elevation gain :	1500 feet
Green Trails map :	No. 177 Chiwaukum Mountains
U.S. Forest Service map :	Wenatchee

A dam built in the 1930s transformed this large and beautiful glacier-carved lake into a reservoir for irrigation and fish hatchery water. Despite the reservoir-type shoreline, the lake is so attractive that families continue to hike here to camp, fish, and swim — especially in early summer, when the reservoir is still full and looks like a pristine lake.

Take U.S. 2 to Leavenworth. On the west side of town, turn right on Icicle Creek Road and drive 8.5 miles. Turn left on Eightmile Creek road No. 7601 and drive 3 miles to Eightmile Creek trail No. 1552, elevation 2900 feet.

Cottonwood trees, wild roses, and dogbane may help take the mind off the sun-exposed steepness of the first ½ mile. The way levels out along an old logging road through a clearcut. But at 1 long mile the path is shaded by a grove of old-growth cedars and silver firs at the entry into

the Alpine Lakes Wilderness. At 1½ miles is a delightful resting place alongside a stream.

At 2½ miles an old burn lets the sun get at you again. Climbing steadily, at 3 miles the trail comes to a small lake that fluctuates according to water needs below. Continue up another ½ mile through a massive red rockslide interspersed with junipers, an eerie place unlike anything before or after on the trail. It's the sort of setting that producers of Western movies like to use. The reward for your hot 3½ miles is Eight-mile Lake, elevation 4461 feet.

Look for the vintage 1930s hand-built stone dam and its ruined, rusty petcock. Swimming here, amid glacier-carved rocks and driftwood logs, can be refreshing — that is to say, *cold*. But after the hot trail, good ... very good. Campsites are on the shoreline to the right.

Eightmile Lake

44. French Creek Campground

Type	: Dayhike or backpack
Difficulty	: Easy for children
Hikable	: Mid-June–October
One way	: 1½ miles
High point	: 2900 feet
Elevation gain	: None
Green Trails map	: No. 177 Chiwaukum Mountains
U.S. Forest Service map	: Wenatchee

A delightful forest walk on a nearly level trail to a campground between two rushing steams, with wading and swimming nearby. Children will find endless places to play near any of the abundant campsites.

Icicle Creek upstream from French Creek Campground

Take U.S. 2 to Leavenworth. On the west side of town turn right on
Icicle Creek road (No. 7600) and drive 17.5 miles to Rock Island Campground. Turn left and stay on road No. 7600, and go another 2 miles to its
end at the Icicle Creek trailhead, elevation 2900 feet.

Icicle Creek trail No. 1551 is a popular entry to the Alpine Lakes
Wilderness, so a family may expect many friendly hikers along the way.
At ¼ mile the way crosses the wilderness boundary and enters an
old-growth forest that rivals those of western Washington.

Easy ups and downs lead in 1 mile to the French Creek bridge, with
campsites on both sides of French Creek.

Children usually vote for the one across the bridge where two
creeks tumble together. But the water is too turbulent for wading here,
so if that's what your kids have in mind, continue along the trail upstream
½ mile to campsites with pools, coves, and sandbars. The river, swift
downstream and up, here flows through a wide, very flat stretch of the
valley. It hardly seems like a river at all, more like a long lake. But the
water *is* moving, though gently. The river is so clear the bottom seems
close — but often it's 10 or more feet deep!

45. Mad River Vacation

Type :	Backpack
Difficulty :	Moderate for children
Hikable :	Mid-July–October
One way to campsites :	2½, 3½, and 6 miles
Loop trip :	12 miles
High point :	6400 feet
Elevation gain :	1250 feet
Green Trails map :	No. 146 Plain
U.S. Forest Service map :	Wenatchee

Here is a glorious place to take children for three days or a week. Streams to wade in, a lake to swim in, loop trips, and viewpoints: all on a plateau where the subalpine forest is richly filled with alpine meadows. The area is seldom used by hikers because it is open to motorcyclists. But during midweek, wheels are scarce. Then, a family can have miles of wild area to itself. Even on weekends, machine riders go home by nightfall. There are countless campsites to choose from; pick the one that suits your pleasure and your speed.

From U.S. 2 between Stevens Pass and Leavenworth turn north on Highway 207 toward Lake Wenatchee State Park. Pass the park and at 4

Patrol cabin near Blue Creek camp

miles, just past the Wenatchee River bridge, go straight ahead on a paved county road. Continue on this road, dodging sideroads to Fish Lake and also the new Chiwawa River road. At 10.5 miles cross the Chiwawa River in the middle of a vacation-home development. Turn north on the old Chiwawa River road No. 61 for 1.6 miles and turn right on road No. 6101. At 7.3 miles from the county road, after a final steep and narrow 2 miles, find Maverick Saddle. An even rougher road, probably best walked, leads 0.3 mile to the trailhead, signed "Mad River trail 1409", elevation 4250 feet.

The first mile of trail has few steep ups and downs. A sturdy bridge spans the Mad River, not much of a "river" here near the headwaters, but a splendid creek. At 2½ miles is the first of many attractive streamside campsites; here you can adjust your ambitions to the capabilities of your children. At 4 miles cross the river on a driftwood log, and at 4½ miles recross on boulders. At 5 miles enter the first of the meadows, and at 6 miles reach unmanned Blue Creek Camp Guard Station, built in the 1920's — an ideal place for a basecamp, elevation 6100 feet.

Day trips abound. Hike 2 miles to Mad Lake on a fairly level trail through meadows and subalpine forest; swimming is good on a small beach at the inlet. Hike to Two Little Lakes at 2½ miles; or loop through Whistling Pig Meadows, named for the colony of marmots. A more strenuous hike is to the top of Cougar Mountain, for panoramic views of forest and mountains. The map will suggest other loops.

Half of the motorcycle drivers on these trails are courteous and will slow down when passing; some of the other half, mainly unsupervised youngsters, whiz by at full speed, using hikers as part of an obstacle course.

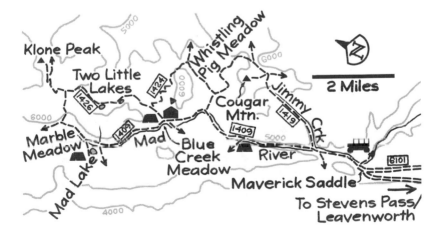

46. Myrtle Lake

Type	:	Dayhike or backpack
Difficulty	:	Moderate for children
Hikable	:	May–November
One way	:	4 miles
High point	:	3800 feet
Elevation gain	:	700 feet
Green Trails map	:	No. 114 Lucerne
U.S. Forest Service map	:	Wenatchee

Along the road beyond Ardenvoir enjoy the pageant of forest re-growth since the great Entiat Fire of 1966. This is the way nature has been restoring itself after disasters for thousands of years. Then hike a gently graded trail along the Entiat River to a peaceful forest lake. In May and June expect to see deer with fawns along the way.

From Entiat on U.S. 97 drive the Entiat River road 38 miles to the road end and the Entiat River trailhead, elevation 3100 feet.

Hikers share trail No. 1400 with motorcyclists and horse riders. This poses no hardship for motorcyclists, but hikers can only hope they do not encounter unsupervised children on the machines. Most of the motorcycle drivers on these trails are courteous and will slow down when passing. Motorcycle traffic is mostly on weekends. During the week a hiker will seldom see more than one or two parties. A hiker-only trail to the lake is scheduled for 1991. The gradual trail passes through a

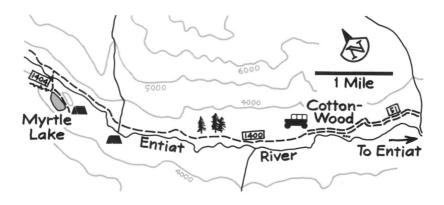

Fawn hidden near Entiat River trail

varied forest of lodgepole pine, fir, and cottonwood. At 2½ miles is a possible campsite, 300 feet downstream from a bridge. At 3½ miles turn left on trail No. 1404 and at 4 miles from the road reach the outlet of Myrtle Lake, elevation 3800 feet.

Some campsites are available at the outlet, but they may be closed. If so, continue another ¼ mile to others at the upper end of the lake.

Deer and fawn

Snoqualmie Pass Highway: West

Interstate 90

47. Tradition Lake Plateau...122
48. Middle Tiger Mountain...124
49. Talapus Lake...126
50. Denny Creek Water Slide...128
51. Franklin Falls...130
52. Lake Annette...132
53. Snow Lake...134

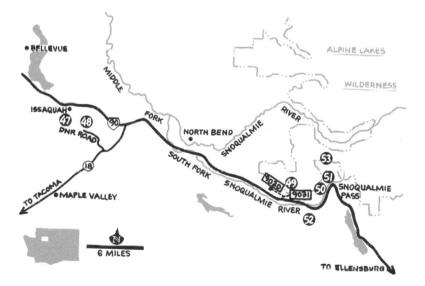

47. Tradition Lake Plateau

Type	:	Dayhike
Difficulty	:	Easy for children
Hikable	:	Year-round
One way	:	1½ miles
High point	:	500 feet
Elevation gain	:	None
Green Trails map	:	None
U.S. Forest Service map	:	None

These three short trail trips with different destinations start from the same parking area; they can be combined or done singly. The Issaquah Alps have become the most popular hiking area near Seattle for two reasons: The trails are less than an hour from any home in King County, so there's no need to fight traffic half the day; and the low elevation means the trails are open year-round. Even on a stormy day in November, a family can still be on a woodland trail for a hike and picnic in surprisingly little time.

Drive I-90 east from Issaquah to Exit 20, signed "High Point." Turn right to the frontage road, and head west on it to the end. Park beside the locked gate.

Walk around the gate and follow the service road ⅓ mile to its intersection with an east-west powerline swath. Walk west on the swath and service road; at ½ mile from the gate you'll come to Tradition Lake. Fed by surface runoff in the rainy season, the lake drops markedly in summer, exposing fields of grass, and reeds, and mint gone wild. The view of West Tiger Mountain rising above the lake is splendid. But to "get into" the lake, take the Round the Lake Trail, circling the wild side. Its two ends are just east and just west of the lake. Keep an eye on a snag just east of the lake — the "Eagle Tree" is a favorite perch of bald eagles. You can also spot great blue herons, various species of ducks, and all manner of little birds. Note the beaver-gnawed stumps; the colony emigrated elsewhere in about 1970. In the low water of fall, two of their old lodges — tangled mounds of logs and branches — can be spotted from the shore. A popular picnic promontory on the west shore has a good view of the lake and the birds.

For more exercise, proceed west from Tradition Lake on the service road to the intersection of the east-west powerline with the north-south powerline and natural gas line. Go south on the north-south service road,

Tradition Lake

and in a short bit turn off on a signed path to Round Lake, a little pond filled with reeds and water lilies, warm enough in early summer for wading. (In late summer the lake dries up.) The tiny wild blackberries growing along this road are delicious.

48. Middle Tiger Mountain

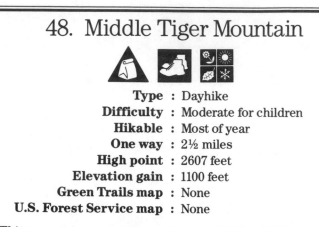

Type : Dayhike
Difficulty : Moderate for children
Hikable : Most of year
One way : 2½ miles
High point : 2607 feet
Elevation gain : 1100 feet
Green Trails map : None
U.S. Forest Service map : None

This mountain summit has a view west to Squak Mountain, Cougar Mountain, the infamous Cedar Hill Landfill, Lake Washington, Bellevue, Seattle, Elliott Bay, Blake, Vashon, Maury and Bainbridge islands, the Tacoma smelter stack and the Narrows, the Olympics, Mount Rainier, and what's left of Mount St. Helens. The trail is open all year and is particularly attractive to families when Snoqualmie Pass trails are snowbound. On the other hand, a family wanting to take a little walk in the snow will find the trip a special joy on those winter days when a promised snowfall has disappointed the kids by not quite getting to the level of their house.

Drive I-90 to Exit 25 and turn right onto Highway 18 for 4.5 miles to Holder Gap (Tiger Summit). Two gravel roads go off north from here,

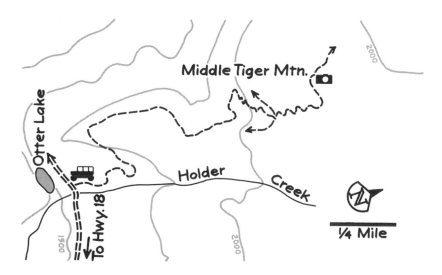

October snow on Middle Tiger Mountain, Mount Rainier in distance

side by side. Take the left-hand one for exactly 2 miles. There is a small pull-off, elevation 1500 feet. The trailhead sign says only "Closed to motorized vehicles." Note, however, the little tab, "TMT," marking this as the famous Tiger Mountain Trail.

The trail sets out in big trees grown up since the logging in the 1920s. Passing enormous stumps, it intersects the Holder Creek railroad grade at ¼ mile. Follow the grade past dead-end spurs where the railroad switchbacked. (The engine pulled ahead on a spur, then backed up the next section of the steep grade, onto another spur, then pulled ahead again.) Watch for ribbon guides tied to tree trunks. At 1¼ miles you come to Karl's Gap, elevation 1910 feet, and a junction; the right fork leads to Wright's Reach, but you must turn left onto another railroad grade.

At 2 miles is the intersection with the West Side Road trail descending left and the Middle Tiger trail climbing to the right. The sign says the summit is ½ mile away but it feels like ¾ mile. Steep! Many trails converge on top — be sure to remember which was yours.

Summit views are worth hours. You can see airplanes taking off and landing at Sea-Tac Airport; ships on the Sound; the towers of downtown Seattle, including the spidery Space Needle; and scores of lakes. In the immediate foreground are West Tiger and East Tiger, each with metal towers on their summits.

49. Talapus Lake

Type	: Dayhike or backpack
Difficulty	: Moderate for children
Hikable	: July–October
One way	: 2 miles
High point	: 3450 feet
Elevation gain	: 1120 feet
Green Trails map	: No. 206 Bandera
U.S. Forest Service map	: Mt. Baker–Snoqualmie

Easy access, a short trail, camping, fishing, and proximity to other woodland lakes are reasons why Talapus is one of the most popular lakes in the greater Snoqualmie Pass area. The trail continues on from Talapus to Olallie and numerous other lowland lakes.

Drive I-90 approximately 15 miles east of North Bend to Bandera Exit 45. Take the overpass to the north side of the highway and follow road No. 9030. At 0.25 mile is a junction with No. 9031; turn right and

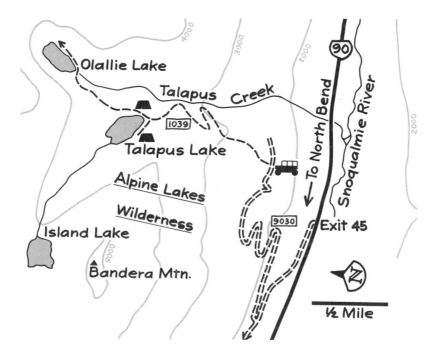

remain on No. 9030 for 3 miles. Find the trailhead at the end of the road, elevation 2600 feet.

Trail No. 1039 begins in a former clearcut with deciduous undergrowth over an old roadbed. The trail climbs gradually in long switchbacks, narrowing as it enters second growth. At 1 mile you come close to a stream with large rocks for resting on. Some can serve as picnic tables if this is your lunch stop.

At 1½ miles the trail levels and enters the Alpine Lakes Wilderness, where you will see enormous old-growth cedars. Watch for wild lily of the valley and the tiny pink bells of twinflower lining the trail. The Swedish botanist Linnaeus, who classified the plant kingdom into genus and species, chose twinflower over all others in the world to bear his name — *Linnaea*.

The trail follows the lake's outlet stream, zigzagging toward and away from it. Some of the zags also make good resting places. Just before the lake there is a fork, with the right trail offering more campsites but the left some good ones as well. At 2 miles comes the first view of the lake set in a deeply wooded basin, elevation 3680 feet. There are at least 15 campsites for the 4000 or more visitors a year this lake receives. The day I was there 16 Cub Scouts were having their fishing lines threaded by their grandfathers. Somebody asked who was going to catch the first fish. All 16 shouted, "I am!"

Talapus Lake

Denny Creek slide area

50. Denny Creek Water Slide

Type	: Dayhike
Difficulty	: Easy for children
Hikable	: May–November
One way	: 1¼ miles
High point	: 2800 feet
Elevation gain	: 500 feet
Green Trails map	: No. 207 Snoqualmie Pass
U.S. Forest Service map	: Mt. Baker–Snoqualmie

On a hot day, this natural water slide can send children out of their minds with glee. One mother with three kids under seven told me they had played three hours — until the sun went down and they began to feel the cold.

Drive I-90 to Denny Creek Exit 47, turn left, and cross the overpass. Turn right on road No. 58, pass Denny Creek Campground, and turn left on road No. 5830 to the signed spur road to the Melakwa Lake trailhead, elevation 2300 feet.

Trail No. 1014 begins in impressive old forest. At ¼ mile it crosses a log bridge children will like. They shortly will be astonished to walk *under* the freeway, to hear cars and trucks rumbling and roaring over their heads, and to peek up through the bridge grates at big black tires rolling by at high speeds. At 1 mile the trail enters the Alpine Lakes Wilderness, and freeway sounds fade away in the distance. A gradual climb along Denny Creek leads to a section of bedrock, elevation 2800 feet, where the water spreads out into the Water Slide.

Water volume may be dangerously torrential in the spring, but in **CAUTION** later months dwindles to a gentle and safe flow. At the same time temperatures rise and kids are attracted like dragonflies. The slide is a wide expanse of bedrock where the creek first narrows to a footstep's width, then widens to slip down the rocky slab. Walk upstream 300 feet to a cascade for children to run under — another exhilarating sensation.

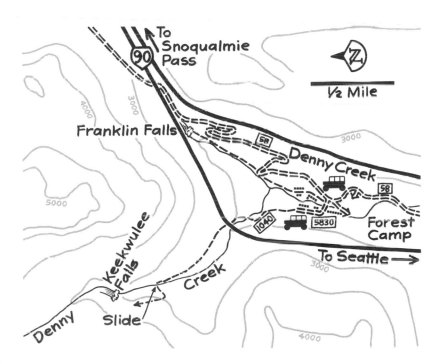

51. Franklin Falls

excellent.
But hold
hands.
Lots of cliffs!

Type	: Dayhike
Difficulty	: Easy for children
Hikable	: July–October
One way	: ¼ mile, ½ mile, or 1 mile
High point	: 2600 feet
Elevation gain	: 100 feet
Green Trails map	: No. 207 Snoqualmie Pass
U.S. Forest Service map	: Mt. Baker–Snoqualmie

See map on page 129

A paradise for kids! Standing beside the 70-foot falls on a warm day, they scream with joy at the cold spray in their face. The gravel bar and the creek into which the water falls usually are crowded with children wading, splashing, playing on the rocks, and "fishing" — as if the fish enjoyed such company! Traffic is loud on the Denny Creek section of freeway directly above, but the kids are oblivious to it.

Four trailheads offer routes varying in length from 1 mile to a scant ¼ mile. Parents with toddlers will opt for the shortest way. Those with older children can make the falls a reward after a longer hike.

Drive I-90 to Exit 47 (Asahel Curtis/Denny Creek). Turn left at the stop sign, crossing the overpasses. At the T turn right. In 0.25 mile turn left on Denny Creek road No. 58. At 2 miles you pass the Denny Creek Campground and at 2.25 miles you reach a junction with road No. 5830, signed "Melakwa Lake Trail"; this is the first of the Franklin Falls trailheads. On the right side of the junction, marked with a wagon wheel, is the historic Snoqualmie Pass Wagon Road, which climbs in 1 mile to Franklin Falls. On the left side, on road No. 5830, is the Franklin Falls trail, also 1 mile in length, starting near the concrete bridge. For a shorter walk, continue up road No. 58 another 0.4 mile for ½ mile to the falls, or continue still another 0.5 mile for the ¼ mile trail, also marked with a wagon wheel.

The sometimes muddy ¼-mile trail joins the wagon road and regular trail, then drops to the falls, the final few feet blasted out of solid rock. There is no guardrail, so children will need supervision and young children will need help. The last 200 yards are surfaced with sharp rocks and could be difficult for toddlers to walk through, so parents should plan to carry them here.

Families blink their eyes in disbelief as they see the falls, creek, large gravel bar, and rock walls for the first time. When I was there on a hot summer day, people were picnicking on blankets and folding chairs, watching children happily engrossed in all manner of watery activities.

Franklin Falls

Lake Annette

52. Lake Annette

Type :	Dayhike or backpack
Difficulty :	Difficult for children
Hikable :	June–October
One way :	4 miles
High point :	3600 feet
Elevation gain :	1400 feet
Green Trails map :	No. 207 Snoqualmie Pass
U.S. Forest Service map :	Mt. Baker–Snoqualmie

A long, steep woodland trail ascends the valley beneath Silver Peak to a cirque lake fed by waterfalls. Kids enjoy splashing around in the many creeks crossed on the way and playing in the lake-outlet stream.

Drive I-90 to Exit 47 (Asahel Curtis/Denny Creek). At the first stop sign turn right, and at the second stop sign turn left. In ½ mile park in the large, paved parking area, elevation 2400 feet. The trail begins on the east side.

For the first ¾ mile the trail ascends old clearcuts to the abandoned Milwaukee Railroad grade — now in the process of becoming a State Parks trail that ultimately will extend to Idaho. A split-log bench is a nice place to rest before starting up a series of steep switchbacks on the western slope of Silver Peak. The trail follows Humpback Creek through stands of large, very old cedar. At one point the "trail" is a log 50 feet long, 3 feet wide, with shallow steps cut into it. The last mile is more gradual, crossing rockslides ornamented in spring by clumps of trillium, glacier lily and Canadian dogwood.

At 4 miles is the lake, elevation 3600 feet. The north shore is designated "day use only." Campsites are on the shoreline beyond the outlet. There is also camping on the ridge on the south side. Trout fishing is said to be very good.

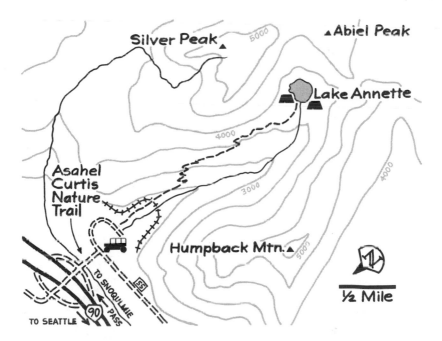

53. Snow Lake

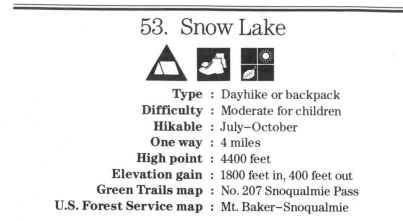

Type : Dayhike or backpack
Difficulty : Moderate for children
Hikable : July–October
One way : 4 miles
High point : 4400 feet
Elevation gain : 1800 feet in, 400 feet out
Green Trails map : No. 207 Snoqualmie Pass
U.S. Forest Service map : Mt. Baker–Snoqualmie

Snow Lake is one of the most popular hikes in the Snoqualmie Pass area. The trail, though, is long and steep for children. My own rebelled at backpacking it when they were 8, 9, and 10, and we bivouacked along the way. But the next day, seeing the lake, they wished they'd kept going and

Snow Lake. Only the chimney of the shelter now remains.

camped there; we returned to do so several times. The rugged and beautiful setting — tall cliffs on one side and vast valley on the other — make it memorable for hikers of all ages.

Drive I-90 to Snoqualmie Pass, turn off on Exit 52, and continue left 2 miles to the parking lot at the Alpental ski area, elevation 3100 feet.

Trail No. 1013, starting on the uphill side of the parking lot, is well maintained throughout and has been partly rebuilt recently. At about 2 miles new short switchbacks have been blasted through rockslides and up through belts of cliffs. The views begin here, down to Source Lake valley and up to Denny, Chair, and Lundin mountains. The track opens out into heather and flowers at Snow Lake saddle, 4400 feet. Peaks along the ridge to the west are, from right to left, Chair Peak, the Tooth, Lundin Peak, and Denny Mountain. (Children will want to see in their shapes the reasons for some of their names.) (Denny, however, has no particular shape; it was named for one of the builders of Seattle.)

From the saddle the sometimes muddy, slippery trail (watch children carefully) drops 400 feet to shores of the lake, elevation 4016 feet, about 4 miles from the parking lot.

The lake is large enough to accommodate a lot of campers, fishermen, photographers, and picnickers, and usually does; over 10,000 hikers a year choose it as their destination. To get away from some of the crowds, and out of the day-use area to the camping area, try the northeast shoreline beyond the outlet. The views one way are down to the vast gulf of the Middle Fork Snoqualmie and in the other across the lake to snowfields extending to the shore.

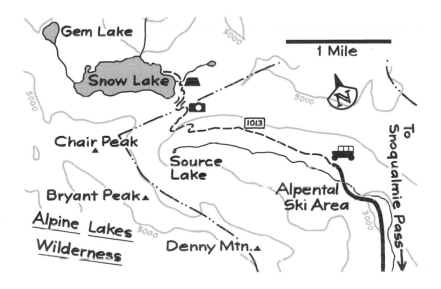

Golden-mantled Ground Squirrel

Snoqualmie Pass Highway: East

Interstate 90

54. Mirror Lake...138
55. Rachel Lake...140
56. Pete Lake...142
57. Hyas Lakes...144

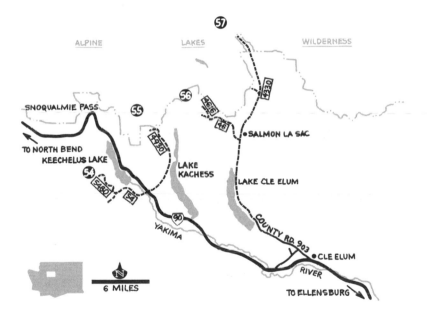

54. Mirror Lake

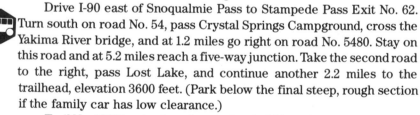

Type	: Dayhike or backpack
Difficulty	: Easy–moderate for children
Hikable	: June–October
One way	: 1 mile
High point	: 4200 feet
Elevation gain	: 600 feet
Green Trails map	: No. 207 Snoqualmie Pass
U.S. Forest Service map	: Wenatchee

This large, clear blue mountain lake lies at the foot of Tinkham Peak. Fishermen, backpacking families, and climbers all find something to enjoy. I saw one fisherman with a 19-inch rainbow trout on his line and a smile on his face. This is a "hikers only" trail, rough in places, muddy in others, with several small streams to cross. Fortunately the trail is short, so little legs should be able to manage.

Drive I-90 east of Snoqualmie Pass to Stampede Pass Exit No. 62. Turn south on road No. 54, pass Crystal Springs Campground, cross the Yakima River bridge, and at 1.2 miles go right on road No. 5480. Stay on this road and at 5.2 miles reach a five-way junction. Take the second road to the right, pass Lost Lake, and continue another 2.2 miles to the trailhead, elevation 3600 feet. (Park below the final steep, rough section if the family car has low clearance.)

Trail No. 1302 begins in a clearcut but in 200 yards enters old-growth forest and at ½ mile reaches shallow Cottonwood Lake, beneath the open slopes of Roaring Ridge. Camping and wading are possible here.

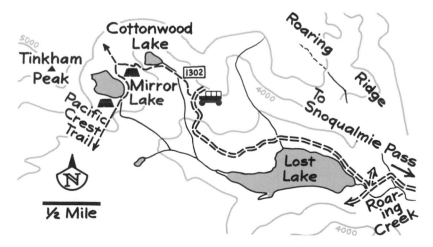

Mirror Lake

Continue another ½ mile, passing large boulders, to Mirror Lake, elevation 4200 feet. Clear and deep, with campsites on both the north and south shores, Mirror Lake reflects whatever a hiker wants to see. Gaze upward 1000 feet to the crags of 5390-foot Tinkam Peak.

55. Rachel Lake

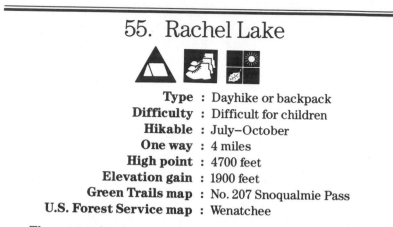

Type : Dayhike or backpack
Difficulty : Difficult for children
Hikable : July–October
One way : 4 miles
High point : 4700 feet
Elevation gain : 1900 feet
Green Trails map : No. 207 Snoqualmie Pass
U.S. Forest Service map : Wenatchee

The outstanding beauty of this exquisite alpine lake carved from the side of Rampart Ridge draws hundreds of hikers every summer weekend, many with small children. Yet this is one of the toughest-to-walk trails in the Cascades, and **definitely not for inexperienced hikers.** The way is clearly marked, but be prepared for rocks, roots, mud, and crawl-over logs. Adults and older kids frequently do Rachel Lake as a dayhike, but it's better as a three-day trip. Carry a stove because campfires are prohibited at all lakes.

Drive I-90 east of Snoqualmie Pass and take the Lake Kachess Exit 62. Follow signs north 5 miles to Lake Kachess Campground, turn left on Box Canyon road No. 4930, and go 4 miles to a junction. Turn left, drive 0.2 mile, and park in the lot at the trailhead, elevation 2800 feet.

Rachel Lake trail No. 1313 leaves the upper side of the parking lot in a forest filled with huckleberries. The tread is rough and narrow, contouring a sidehill toward Box Canyon Creek. At ½ mile the trail improves somewhat, entering the Alpine Lakes Wilderness. You'll find campsites at 1 mile. Follow the trail along the creek for the next 2 miles, always within sight and sound of it. At 2½ miles the trail crosses several streams and switchbacks uphill beside a waterfall, a good place to rest and cool hands and faces, in anticipation of the next 1½ miles — "the cruel mile" — that will climb 1300 feet.

At about 3 miles the trail passes under a waterfall — another good resting point, with a free shower thrown in. (Some children go wild, soaking heads, feet, or even standing in the falls.) From here, the trail is at its worst, climbing over rocks, boulders, and roots, and up streambeds, until at 4 miles, the grade abruptly levels out at deep blue Rachel Lake, elevation 4700 feet. Numerous campsites are scattered on both sides of the outlet stream.

If your children (and you) survive the trail to Rachel Lake, the

Rachel Lake

middle day of a three-day trip can be the best. From the lake outlet climb the boot-beaten trail to the right, gaining 600 feet up the very steep mountainside to the broad saddle between Rampart Ridge and Alta Mountain. Take the trail left an up-and-down ½ mile to Rampart Lakes, a magnificent chain set in glacier-scoured bedrock bowls. Children can wade, swim, and throw rocks; parents can sketch or photograph these picture-perfect settings.

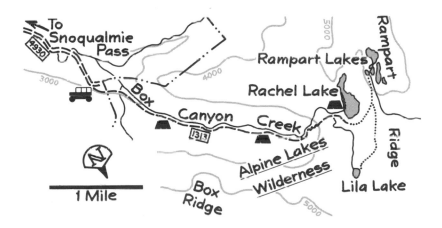

56. Pete Lake

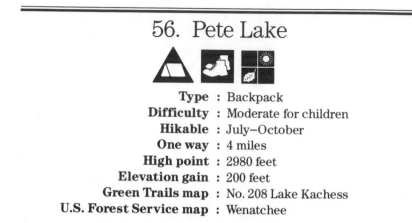

Type : Backpack
Difficulty : Moderate for children
Hikable : July–October
One way : 4 miles
High point : 2980 feet
Elevation gain : 200 feet
Green Trails map : No. 208 Lake Kachess
U.S. Forest Service map : Wenatchee

Large, woodland Pete Lake makes a popular family campsite at the end of a gentle trail through old-growth forest. Children will joyfully throw sticks and stones in three or four creeks along the way. At the lake they can also wade and swim, because the water, while not warm, is also not ice cold. Because there is no special turnaround point, this hike is best for an overnight trip.

Drive I-90 east of Snoqualmie Pass and turn off on Exit 80, signed "Salmon la Sac–Roslyn." Follow the county road, through Roslyn and Ronald, and along Cle Elum Lake, for 15 miles. Turn left on Cooper Lake

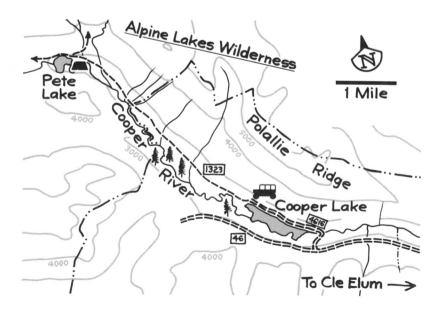

Pete Lake and horse barn.

road No. 46, go 4.7 miles, and turn right on road No. 4616. Cross Cooper Creek on a cement bridge, pass a campground and boat launch, and 1.8 miles from road No. 46 is the trailhead, elevation 2800 feet.

Cooper River trail No. 1323 joins a lakeshore path and winds through virgin timber and undergrowth. At about 4 miles is a giant rockslide and the last little climb before reaching the lake, elevation 2980 feet.

To the west of the lake are exciting views of Overcoat and Bears Breast mountains. I have pictures of my three children beneath the peaks sitting on a log eating their breakfast porridge like the three bears.

Hyas Lake

57. Hyas Lakes

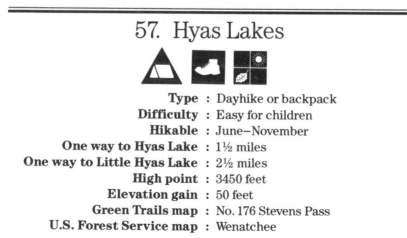

Type	: Dayhike or backpack
Difficulty	: Easy for children
Hikable	: June–November
One way to Hyas Lake	: 1½ miles
One way to Little Hyas Lake	: 2½ miles
High point	: 3450 feet
Elevation gain	: 50 feet
Green Trails map	: No. 176 Stevens Pass
U.S. Forest Service map	: Wenatchee

Two large forested lakes — very popular, and with campsites almost beyond counting — wait at the end of a gradual trail through fine old timber. From camps near the shores of either Hyas or Little Hyas lakes, or the swampy, reed-filled area between the two, searches can be made for frogs, newts, and salamanders. Cathedral Rock rises a striking 6000 feet above the west shores.

Drive I-90 east of Snoqualmie Pass and turn at Exit 80, signed "Salmon la Sac–Roslyn." Go 3 miles and turn left on county road No. 903. Wind through the old mining town of Roslyn and pass Lake Cle Elum, a small natural lake made into a huge reservoir whose level fluctuates. At 17 miles from Roslyn, just beyond the Salmon la Sac Guard Station, go right on unpaved road No. 4330. Drive 15 more miles to its end and Hyas Lakes trail No. 1376, elevation 3400 feet.

The trail is nearly flat and so wide that families can walk abreast. Three or four creeks can be difficult to cross in the high waters of early summer, but later make good spots to rest or play. An easy 1½ miles leads to the larger of the two Hyas Lakes. Another easy mile more reaches Little Hyas Lake, elevation 3450 feet.

Campsites are scattered along both lakes. The first lakeshore camp has the best swimming beach, but you must arrive very early (preferably Friday evening) to have a chance to get it. Note that the sandy beach ends in an abrupt drop-off, so keep a careful eye on non-swimmers. Some camps at Little Hyas Lake are large enough for several congenial families camping together. Downed logs and the exposed roots of enormous old trees provide play places for children and their real or imaginary friends.

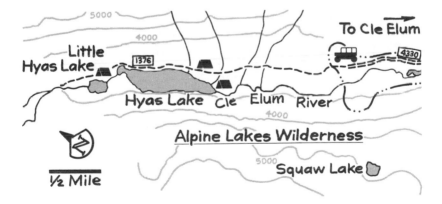

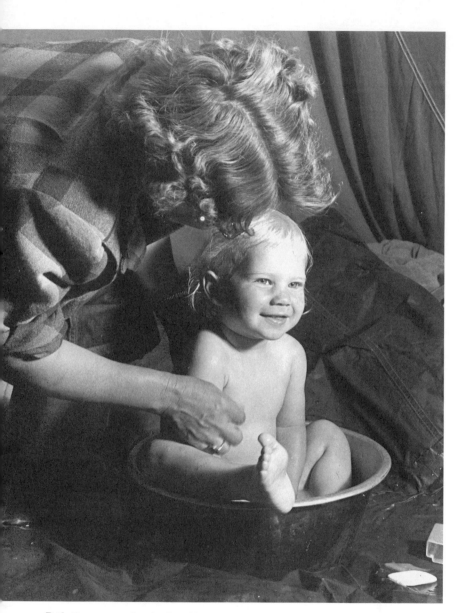

Bath time, even when backpacking

Chinook Pass Highway: West

U.S. 410

58. Carbon Glacier...148
59. Eunice Lake...150
60. Spray Park...152
61. Glacier Basin...154
62. Shadow Lake Trail...156
63. Burroughs Mountain...158

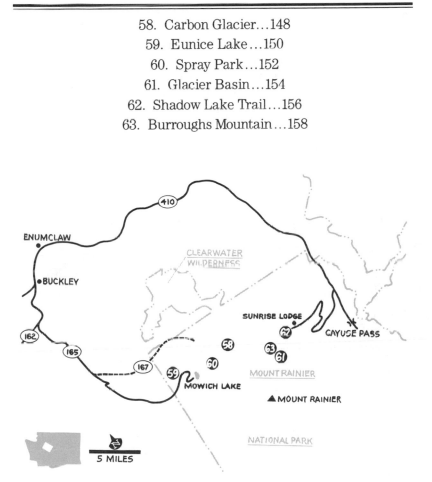

58. Carbon Glacier

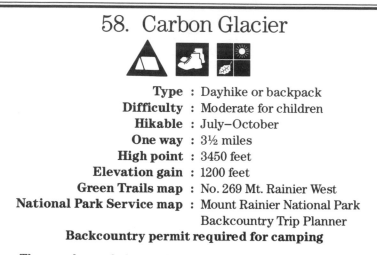

Type	:	Dayhike or backpack
Difficulty	:	Moderate for children
Hikable	:	July–October
One way	:	3½ miles
High point	:	3450 feet
Elevation gain	:	1200 feet
Green Trails map	:	No. 269 Mt. Rainier West
National Park Service map	:	Mount Rainier National Park
		Backcountry Trip Planner

Backcountry permit required for camping

The gently graded woodland trail follows Ipsut Creek and the Carbon River to its impressive source, the snout of Carbon Glacier itself.

Rock-strewn Carbon Glacier

(Bring binoculars to view nearby crevasses and overhanging cornices.) Though the trail is wide and not steep, some areas are rocky and rough from the annual spring floods. People with short legs and small feet will have trouble with footing. The hike includes a swaying suspension bridge. Children love the giddy crossing, especially when their parents get dizzy.

Drive State Highway 410 east from Tacoma or south from Enumclaw to the town of Buckley. From the southern outskirts of town follow state highways 162 and 165 south through Wilkeson and Carbonado. Shortly after crossing the Fairfax Bridge, high above the canyon of the Carbon River, come to a fork. Stay left, following signs to the Carbon River entrance to Mount Rainier National Park. Enter the park and drive to the road end at Ipsut Creek Campground, elevation 2350 feet. Sometimes this road washes out, so early in the season call to Mount Rainier National Park headquarters and check before starting. (When the road is washed out, or closed at the park entrance, as it usually is in winter, it makes a glorious woodland walk in itself.)

The trail starts at the upper end of the campground. Trees are old and massive. Look for very large Douglas firs, western hemlocks, and also Alaska cedars, distinguishable from Western red cedars because their branches droop more. Not only is the forest floor moss-carpeted, but the trees themselves are festooned with moss. Prepare for a gasp at 2½ miles — your first glimpse of Mount Rainier. Expect a majestic view up the Carbon Glacier to Liberty Ridge and Curtis Ridge. Deer and bear are occasionally seen below and above the creek.

At 3 miles you pass Carbon River Camp at the tumbling waters of Cataract Creek. Continue beside the Carbon River to the swaying suspension bridge, which lifts hikers high above the "rock-milk"-laden stream tumbling down from the glacier, which ground up all those rocks to make the "milk." On the other side continue ½ mile to the vicinity of the glacier snout. Far enough.

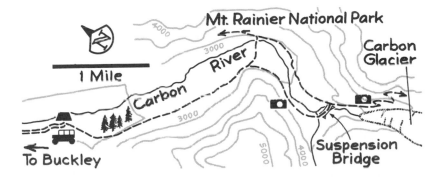

59. Eunice Lake

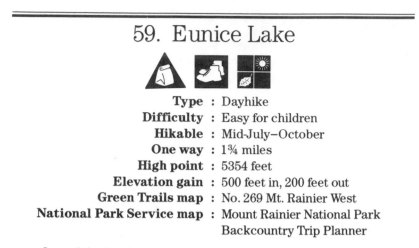

Type :	Dayhike
Difficulty :	Easy for children
Hikable :	Mid-July–October
One way :	1¾ miles
High point :	5354 feet
Elevation gain :	500 feet in, 200 feet out
Green Trails map :	No. 269 Mt. Rainier West
National Park Service map :	Mount Rainier National Park Backcountry Trip Planner

One of the loveliest alpine lakes in Mount Rainier National Park is reached by a short hike from Mowich Lake. Above Eunice a steep, short trail climbs to the Tolmie Peak lookout. Children are perfectly enchanted by Eunice Lake, however. One hot day I heard a mother ask who wanted to climb to the summit; four children playing on the shore replied in unison, "Not me!"

Follow highways 162 and 165 through Wilkeson and Carbonado, past the high, narrow bridge over the Carbon River, to the fork beyond (Hike 58). Keep right at the fork and follow the road to its end at Mowich Lake, elevation 4929 feet. Park along the road where it crosses the pass from which Mowich Lake is first visible. The trail to Eunice Lake heads north from the road. If there is no parking at the pass, continue downhill to the road-end parking lot at the lake and pick up the trail there.

Actually, two trails depart from the parking lot. The trail to Spray Park (Hike 60) heads downhill from the walk-in campsite on the south side of Mowich Lake near the outlet stream. The trail to Eunice Lake — here, a short segment of the Wonderland Trail — begins on the opposite side of the parking lot. It rounds the lakeshore through old-growth noble and silver firs and Alaska cedars, then parallels the nearby road to the pass mentioned above. At 1¼ miles is a junction. The Wonderland Trail goes right over Ipsut Pass. Your way goes left on the Eunice Lake trail, but take the time to walk the Wonderland Trail a few feet to look out over the Carbon River valley.

The trail to Eunice Lake drops 100 feet to skirt a cliff and then climbs ½ mile to berry-filled meadows and the lake, 5354 feet. Mount Rainier is suddenly and vastly apparent.

If children can bear to leave the waterplay, the 1-mile hike to Tolmie

Eunice Lake and Mount Rainier

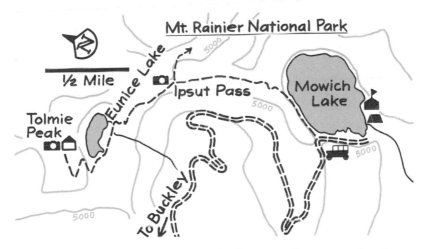

Peak lookout (600-foot elevation gain) gives grandly spectacular views. Look north for Mount Baker, east for Glacier Peak, and almost reach out to touch Rainier. Plan the hike for a warm day in late summer when berries are ripe; cool off by wading or dunking in the lake.

Mount Rainier and field of avalanche lilies in Spray Park

60. Spray Park

Type	:	Dayhike or backpack
Difficulty	:	Moderate for children
Hikable	:	Mid-July–October
One way	:	2¾ miles
High point	:	5700 feet
Elevation gain	:	1100 feet in, 300 feet out
Green Trails map	:	No. 269 Mt. Rainier West
National Park Service map	:	Mount Rainier National Park Backcountry Trip Planner

Backcountry permits required for camping

Some of the most exquisite flower meadows on the north side of Mount Rainier National Park can be attained for a small expenditure of energy. Views of "The Mountain" above fields of avalanche lilies here are unforgettable. Though there is no camping in Spray Park, families can camp in the woods at Eagles Roost, then do the higher day trips above.

From Buckley drive to the parking lot at Mowich Lake (Hike 59).

Start from the walk-in campsite south of the lake. The beginning is on the Wonderland Trail, which drops ½ mile to a junction. Go left on the Spray Park trail, wide and gently graded, through a forest of immense old-growth noble and silver fir. At 1½ miles stop to peer over Eagle Cliff. Children will be astonished to find themselves on top of a precipice with views across a deep valley to the snouts of the Mowich and Russell glaciers.

Just beyond is the campsite at Eagles Roost. At 2 miles a side trail goes off ¼ mile to Spray Falls — well worth the trip to eat lunch with more views, in a cooling mist from the falls.

Back on the trail, the last ¾ mile switchbacks steeply upward 600 feet to the meadows of Spray Park, elevation 5700 feet.

Here one can see avalanche lilies in June; lupine, anemones, and paintbrush in mid-July; and asters and gentian in August. Blueberries continue into September. Some of the flower meadows are fringed with small subalpine firs that are encroaching, but nowadays the timberline is here, at the meadow edge, and as hikers continue upward, the views open wider and wider, until trees disappear altogether.

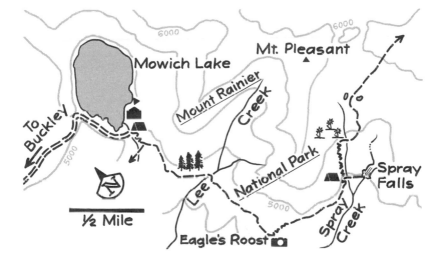

61. Glacier Basin

Type	: Dayhike or backpack
Difficulty	: Difficult for children
Hikable	: Mid-July–October
One way	: 3½ miles
High point	: 6000 feet
Elevation gain	: 1700 feet
Green Trails map	: No. 270 Mt. Rainier East
National Park Service map	: Mount Rainier National Park
	Backcountry Trip Planner

Backcountry permits required for camping

The meadow at Glacier Basin is a marmot metropolis. Elk graze in the lush grass; goats frequently amble on the ridge above, sometimes by the dozens. But perhaps the most exciting wildlife is the ubiquitous mountain climber, sure to be seen on summer weekends, usually in enormous numbers, on his or her way to or from the summit of Mount Rainier. There are also the ghosts of the prospectors who began digging here at the turn of the century, and now have vanished completely.

Drive U.S. 410 east from Enumclaw toward Chinook Pass. Enter Mount Rainier National Park, continue to the White River Entrance Station, then go 5 miles more, cross the White River, and turn left on the White River Campground road. Go to the road's end, elevation 4300 feet.

The trail begins at the upper end of the last campground loop on a miners' road, used until the 1950s, beside the glacier-silted Inter Fork White River. Much of the way the old roadbed is wide enough for two to walk abreast. Children may see evidence of porcupine scratches low down on older tree trunks. The trail climbs alongside the Emmons Glacier moraine. At 1 mile a side trail to the left crosses Inter Fork and climbs to a viewpoint of the snout of the Emmons Glacier and out over the immense expanse of ice, strewn with enormous rocks from the avalanche that swept across the glacier from Little Tahoma in 1964.

Beyond the side trail the path narrows to true trail, climbing through forest and rejoining the old road at about 2¼ miles. At 2½ miles is a switchback; look for some wheels and piles of rotten boards, the remains of the Starbo Mine's power generator. The steep final mile levels out at last in Glacier Basin at 3½ miles, elevation 6000 feet. Campsites are everywhere, if you choose to stay.

Watch for summit parties loaded with high-tech equipment for

Marmot beside the Glacier Basin trail

climbing glaciers. Continue into the meadowy basin and watch for hoary
marmots. Children can whistle to them and think they are being an-
swered by a network of marmot cousins; in fact, each "extended family"
has a lookout marmot posted, usually on a big rock. They pick up and
pass on other whistles whenever one spots an intruder who resembles a
bear or coyote.

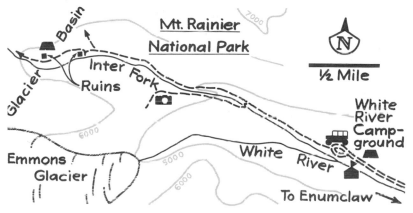

62. Shadow Lake Trail

Type :	Dayhike
Difficulty :	Easy for children
Hikable :	Mid-July–October
One way :	1½ miles
High point :	6100 feet
Elevation gain :	200 feet in, 200 feet out
Green Trails map :	No. 270 Mt. Rainier East
National Park Service map :	Mount Rainier National Park Backcountry Trip Planner

Flowers, meadows, ground squirrels, marmots, Christmas trees in a parkland setting, plus a shallow lake for wading — all this with your choice of taking a gated road or a delightful trail. A spectacular viewpoint of the Emmons Glacier can be thrown in.

Drive U.S. 410 east from Enumclaw to the White River Entrance Station of Mount Rainier National Park. From the station drive to the end of the road at the Sunrise Visitor Center parking lot, elevation 6400 feet.

Find the gated service road at the southwest corner of the parking lot. Either walk the sometimes too-hot road or the usually cool, shadowed trail. Both start at the same place, both distances are the same, both lose 200 feet, and both end up in a walk-in campground. The trail is by far the more pleasant. It has some ups and downs, but also the best flowers, and the tread is smooth. Views of Rainier are good. At 1½

Hikers on Shadow Lake trail

miles you reach Shadow Lake, amid meadows and neatly trimmed subalpine trees. Explain to the kids how they are shaped by nature to shed the heavy winter snow.

For most people the lake is far enough. Children love wading and catching the polliwogs and frogs. (How the frogs feel about being caught again and again has not been recorded.) Should your family be ready to see still more, ½ mile farther and 300 feet higher is one of the most spectacular vistas of the Emmons Glacier. Follow the trail ⅛ mile to the walk-in campground and follow the Burroughs Mountain trail to the first viewpoint (Hike 63).

63. Burroughs Mountain

Type	: Dayhike
Difficulty	: Moderate for children
Hikable	: Mid-July–September
One way to First Burroughs	: 1¼ miles
One way to Second Burroughs	: 1¾ miles
High point	: 7400 feet
Elevation gain	: 900 feet
Green Trails map	: No. 270 Mt. Rainier East
National Park Service map	: Mount Rainier National Park Backcountry Trip Planner

See map on page 156

Burroughs Mountain is so close to Mount Rainier's gigantic north side glaciers it seems to run right into them — in fact, it looks down on their lower paths to crevasses and around the corner to the base of Willis Wall. Some seasons, snowpatches linger late on the trail and are very dangerous, so call ahead to ask the ranger if the snow is gone. Sometimes they are perilous even when the trail is legally "open". Aside from that the trail is wide, smooth, and well maintained. There may be an icy wind, so be sure to carry extra clothing for the summit.

Drive to Sunrise Visitor Center (Hike 62), elevation 6400 feet. Two trails from the parking lot go to First Burroughs Mountain. Each has a steep, dangerous snowpatch that seldom melts before August and some years not at all. When the snow is gone, the upper trail past Frozen Lake is the easier, but the snow often stays longer on this north-facing slope. The lower route past Sunrise Camp loses 200 feet before climbing, but its snow faces south, and thus melts earlier.

Sunrise Camp Route: From the southwest corner of the parking lot take the service road or the trail to Sunrise Camp. Both ways are about 1¼ miles and lose some 200 feet. At the campsites, find the trail, which climbs steeply upwards to Burroughs Mountain. In ¼ mile is a magnificent overlook of the White River and Emmons Glacier. Views get even better the higher one goes on the trail, which climbs 900 feet to First Burroughs and then joins the Frozen Lake trail.

Frozen Lake Route: From the picnic area behind the restrooms the trail climbs steeply up Sourdough Ridge, gaining 400 feet. Stay left at the trail junction to reach Frozen Lake (actually a reservoir) and a junction of five trails. Take the trail on the left and follow it up along the rocky

Mount Rainier from First Burroughs Mountain

slopes of First Burroughs Mountain. Round a slope of andesite lava slabs and pass (or turn back at) the late snowfield, and in ¾ mile attain the plateau summit of First Burroughs Mountain, 7300 feet, and the junction with the Sunrise Camp trail.

First Burroughs, a plateau as flat as a surveyor's table, overlooks the Emmons, Carbon, and Winthrop glaciers. The reason it has so little plant life is that the moisture from rain and snowmelt drain underground, creating an arid condition here. The result is true tundra — a special alpine plant community like that in northern Alaska. The scattered plants have a hard time surviving, and must not be stepped on. Children (and parents) should stay on the marked paths to give them a fighting chance.

The trail dips a little, then climbs again, and ½ mile from the First Burroughs junction reaches the summit of Second Burroughs Mountain, elevation 7400 feet. Here the views expand outward to Grand Park, Moraine Park, Frozen Lake, and Glacier Basin; and upward to Interglacier, Steamboat Prow, and the chains of summit climbers moving slowly up or down. Tell the children a glacier is a great river of ice filled with crevasses caused both by the flow of ice moving more swiftly in the center than on the sides, and by the resistance of boulders underneath.

Spider web covered with dew

Chinook Pass Highway: East

U.S. 410

64. Sheep Lake...162
65. Naches Peak Loop...164
66. Dewey Lakes...166
67. Blankenship Lakes...168
68. Twin Sisters Lakes...170
69. William O. Douglas Wilderness Vacation...172

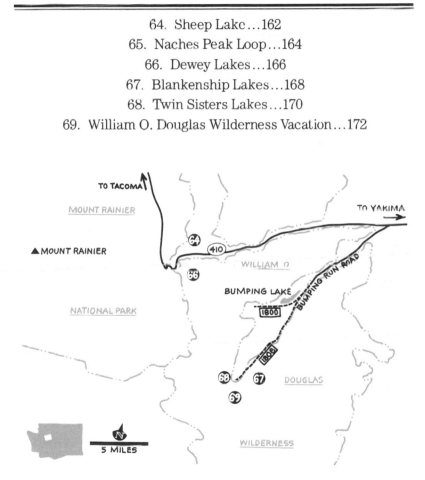

64. Sheep Lake

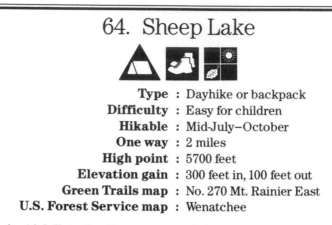

Type :	Dayhike or backpack
Difficulty :	Easy for children
Hikable :	Mid-July–October
One way :	2 miles
High point :	5700 feet
Elevation gain :	300 feet in, 100 feet out
Green Trails map :	No. 270 Mt. Rainier East
U.S. Forest Service map :	Wenatchee

A sidehill trail offers an easy stroll through meadowland to a delightful lake surrounded on three sides by cliffs. (I talked to a mother who was proud that her three-year-old had walked three-quarters of the way, and to a five-year-old who had walked all the way, carrying his own small pack.) Kids love catching polliwogs along the shallow shoreline.

Drive U.S. 410 east from Enumclaw to the parking area at Chinook Pass summit, just outside the Mount Rainier National Park entrance,

Sheep Lake

elevation 5432 feet. Find the Pacific Crest Trailhead to the north of the old wooden overpass.

The trail heads north, paralleling the highway and dropping slightly. The trail was blasted into the steep and rocky hillside, so sometimes it's a little rough. This is part of the Pacific Crest Trail, open to horses, and while they are few, meeting a horse on a narrow trail on the steep hillside is very uncomfortable. There is no way the horse can turn around or back up, so the hiker must do so. At 1¼ miles the trail diverges from the highway, the tread becomes smooth, and a gentle ascent through a little meadow with trees leads to Sheep Lake, elevation 5700 feet.

Campsites are scattered around the shore and above the outlet. For better views, although not of Mount Rainier, hike another mile to Sourdough Gap.

Naches Peak Loop trail and Mount Rainier

65. Naches Peak Loop

Type	:	Dayhike
Difficulty	:	Moderate for children
Hikable	:	Mid-July–October
Loop trip	:	5 miles
High point	:	5800 feet
Elevation gain	:	600 feet
Green Trails maps	:	No. 270 Mt. Rainier East, No. 271 Bumping Lake
National Park Service map	:	Mount Rainier National Park Backcountry Trip Planner

A dream hike for families. Children love picking berries along the easy trail and playing in the warm, shallow pond at its highest point. Parents will be inspired by the magnificence of the views. Small ponds and an early-season waterfall invite children to a ducking of some kind or, on a hot day, a full showerbath. The trail is gently graded, and except for early-season snowpatches, is a cinch for toddlers. Older kids may engage in snowball warfare.

Drive U.S. 410 east from Enumclaw through Mount Rainier National Park to the Chinook Pass summit. Drive under the wooden overpass to the large parking area and park just outside the park boundary. Elevation, 5434 feet.

Walk across the overpass, then contour the east side of Naches Peak and enter the William O. Douglas Wilderness. You pass a small pond, and climb over a 5800-foot spur ridge.

The way then drops a bit, enters Mount Rainier National Park, and at 1½ miles comes to a junction. The left fork drops to Dewey Lake (Hike 66). Go right, into a grand sprawl of alpine meadows. The stupefying views of Mount Rainier are framed by flowers, subalpine trees, and clumps of beargrass. Look for pink Indian paintbrush, gray-bearded anemones gone to seed (Old Man of the Mountain), lavender phlox, white valerian, and golden arnica. At 2 miles is a small, warm lake that cries out to be circled, tested, and waded in. From here the continuation of the loop is all downhill to Tipsoo Lakes. The driver (only) must then walk up the highway ¼ mile, gaining 150 feet, to the parked car.

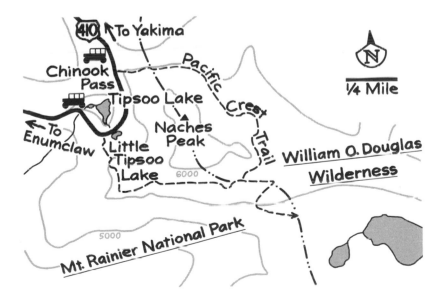

66. Dewey Lakes

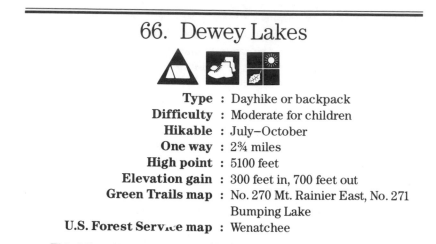

Type	:	Dayhike or backpack
Difficulty	:	Moderate for children
Hikable	:	July–October
One way	:	2¾ miles
High point	:	5100 feet
Elevation gain	:	300 feet in, 700 feet out
Green Trails map	:	No. 270 Mt. Rainier East, No. 271
		Bumping Lake
U.S. Forest Service map	:	Wenatchee

This hike offers a little bit of everything kids love. To begin, the trail crosses the highway on an old wooden overpass. What child can resist the appeal of a high traverse over the highway? There are also summer snowbanks for sliding and snowballing, a waterfall, and two wading and swimming lakes to camp by.

From Enumclaw or Yakima drive U.S. 410 to Chinook Pass to a parking lot just outside the entrance to Mount Rainier National Park, elevation 5434 feet.

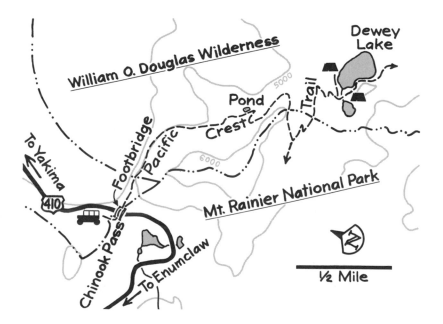

Unnamed tarn on the Pacific Crest trail to Dewey Lakes

Walk across the overpass bridge and head south on the Pacific Crest Trail, contouring the slope of Naches Peak. You enter the William O. Douglas Wilderness and pass an unnamed pond — be sure to check it for polliwogs. There are many early-summer snowpatches, so prepare for snowball fights. (The snow generally lasts until the start of August.) At about 1 mile watch for a waterfall on the right, where on a warm day in early summer a cooling showerbath may be taken.

The trail is mostly smooth, with easy 10-percent grade climbing to a 5800-foot high point. At 1½ miles the Naches Peak loop trail (Hike 40) goes right. You also have your first good look at Mount Rainier. Keep left on the Pacific Crest Trail, signed "Dewey Lakes." Descend 700 feet on long switchbacks with occasional views of Rainier. The destination is a meadow between Upper and Lower Dewey lakes, 5100 feet.

If you want to linger overnight, excellent campsites lie around both lakeshores. The flower fields are famous when in full bloom, which in an average year is mid-July to early August.

67. Blankenship Lakes

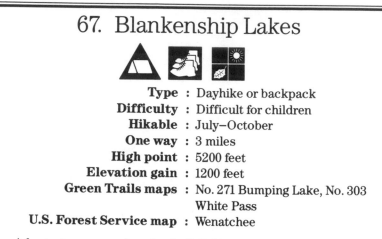

Type : Dayhike or backpack
Difficulty : Difficult for children
Hikable : July–October
One way : 3 miles
High point : 5200 feet
Elevation gain : 1200 feet
Green Trails maps : No. 271 Bumping Lake, No. 303
White Pass
U.S. Forest Service map : Wenatchee

A huge grassy meadow, football-field size, lies on the way to lovely Blankenship Lakes. The first — and longest — lake is one of the most attractive alpine lakes in the William O. Douglas Wilderness. However, the trail, heavily used by horses, is steep and eroded, and thus not easy for young children.

Drive U.S. 410 either west from Yakima or 19 miles east from Chinook Pass and turn south on the Bumping River road. Go 11 miles to Bumping Lake, then continue on road No. 1800 another 2.5 miles to a

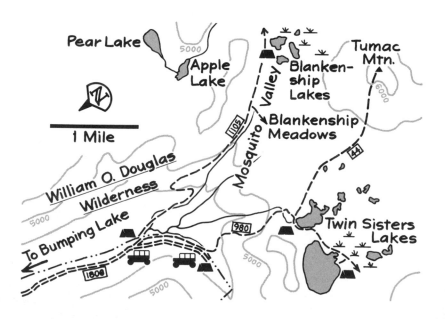

junction. Go straight ahead on road No. 1808 for 6.3 miles to the first Twin Sisters Lakes trailhead, elevation 4100 feet.

Walk a few feet on the Twin Sisters Lakes trail to the sign "Blankenship Meadows 1½ miles." Don't believe it. It's at least a mile longer. Cross the rocky rubble left by a flood, and enter the William O. Douglas Wilderness. The trail is steep, and consists mostly of ruts, roots, and quagmires. But be thankful for one thing — it is in cool forest. At 2½ miles the grade gentles into Blankenship Meadows, one of the largest meadows in the Cascades — the surface of an ancient lava flow. The way through the meadow is marked by occasional posts and a deep trough gouged out by horses' hoofs. The trail at last enters subalpine forest and descends slightly to the largest of the Blankenship Lakes, elevation 5268 feet, a long 3 miles from the road. Small meadows ring the shores. During the dry season the lake lowers a bit and the outlet dries up.

Tumac Mountain is reflected in the still waters. ("Tumac" is not an Indian name. Two early sheepherders here were Scots — "Macs." So, "Two Mac Mountain.") A map will help you locate more lakes. As a matter of fact, you will need a map that uses trail numbers just to understand the signs in this area, because they give *only* numbers, not names. The map shows it is possible to finish this trip as a loop by going back by way of Little Twin Sister Lake trail. However, the first mile of that trail is so steep and badly eroded that the recommended route is to return the way you came.

Blankenship Meadows

68. Twin Sisters Lakes

Type	: Dayhike or backpack
Difficulty	: Easy for children
Hikable	: Mid-July–October
One way to Little Twin	: 1¾ miles
One way to Big Twin	: 2¼ miles
High point	: 5200 feet
Elevation gain	: 900 feet
Green Trails maps	: No. 271 Bumping Lake, No. 303 White Pass
U.S. Forest Service map	: Wenatchee

See map on page 168

These two large jewellike lakes lie close together on a well-graded trail, close enough to the road for a day trip, but delightful enough to deserve an overnight at one of the many excellent campsites. They are among the largest mountain lakes in the state, and are protected as part of the William O. Douglas Wilderness. In season the alpine flowers are wonderful; blueberries, huckleberries, and ground whortleberries ripen in late summer.

Take U.S. 410 west from Yakima or 19 miles east from Chinook Pass and turn south on the Bumping River road. Go 11 miles to Bumping Lake and then follow road No. 1800 to the junction with road No. 1808 (Hike 67). Keep straight ahead, following No. 1808 past the first Twin Sisters Lakes trailhead and at 7 miles reach the second Twin Sisters Lakes trailhead at Deep Creek Campground, elevation 4300 feet.

The trail is kept in good condition. The first half has a gentle grade; the last half steepens to Little Twin Sister Lake at 1¾ miles, with its sandy beaches, and lovely inlets and coves. The best campsites are near the outlet, elevation 5200 feet.

The trail proceeds ½ mile, losing 50 feet, to Big Twin Sister Lake, elevation 5152 feet. Twice the size of the little sister, it too has great campsites at the outlet. Between the two lakes are numerous frog ponds and, of course, flowers by the thousands. Horses' hoofs have trampled parts of the trail into mire.

For a panoramic view of the William O. Douglas Wilderness, over-nighters can climb to the old lookout site atop Tumac Mountain, an extinct (we hope) volcano. Cross the outlet of Little Twin Sister Lake and follow trail No. 44. In ⅓ mile keep right at a junction and continue 2

Big Twin Sister Lake

miles on the Tumac Mountain trail. The trail starts on a gentle grade and
then steepens as it spirals up to the 6340-foot summit, 1200 feet above
the lake.

69. William O. Douglas Wilderness Vacation

Type : Backpack
Difficulty : Moderate for children
Hikable : July–October
Loop trip : 30 miles
High point : 5400 feet
Elevation gain : 2500 feet
Green Trails maps : No. 303 White Pass, No. 271 Bumping Lake
U.S. Forest Service map : Wenatchee

It's such beautiful country, and there are so many delightful spots, we recommend it for a week-long vacation. Because it is horse country, some sections of the trail are a quagmire, especially early in the season when trails are soft. Justice William O. Douglas spent much of his leisure time — from boyhood until he was past 70 years of age — exploring this area, preserved now for us and our children. You may want to set up a base camp at Twin Sisters Lakes, then visit other nearby lakes each day. Or, in early season, when water is plentiful, this trip can be done as a grand loop. However, when water is plentiful, so are mosquitoes, thousands and thousands of them, each with an enormous appetite.

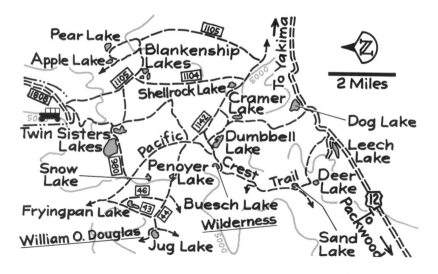

Grouse

For that reason, even though the peak of the flower season may be past, mid-August to September is the most pleasant time to backpack in this area.

For the loop, drive to the second Twin Sisters trailhead (Hike 68). Unload the packs, drive back to the first Twin Lakes parking lot, leave the car, and walk ¾ mile back up to the packs.

Hike the 1½ miles to Little Twin Sister Lake (Hike 68), your first camp. From there, take trail No. 980 downhill 2 miles to the Pacific Crest Trail, turn north, and go 1 mile. Turn left on trail No. 43 and go ½ mile to a camp at Frying Pan Lake. For the third stage, go south on trail No. 46, and turn on No. 44. Pass Penoyer Lake, rejoin the Pacific Crest Trail, and follow it south to camp at Dumbbell Lake, 5 miles. The next camp is a scant 3 miles away on trail No. 1142 to Shellrock Lake. Next go 7 miles (long for children) on trails No. 1142 and No. 1104 to Blankenship Lakes (Hike 67). (From this camp you can take a 3½-mile day trip to Apple and Pear lakes.) The final stage is 3 miles, crossing Blankenship Meadows and back down to the road. The loop covers a total distance, with side trips, of less than 30 miles and an elevation gain of about 2500 feet.

If the loop is not practical, you can still explore lakes and ponds beyond counting. From Twin Lakes, Fryingpan Lake, surrounded by meadows, is a must. Other possibilities are Jug, Snow, Penoyer, Dumbbell, and Cramer lakes. They're like eating popcorn ... once you start you can't stop. But each lake has a character all its own.

Mink

Mount Rainier National Park Highway

State Route 760

70. Bertha May and Granite Lakes...176
71. High Rock...178
72. Lake Christine...180
73. Indian Henry's Hunting Ground...182
74. Lake George...184
75. Klapatche Park...186
76. Comet Falls — Van Trump Park...188
77. Pinnacle Saddle...190

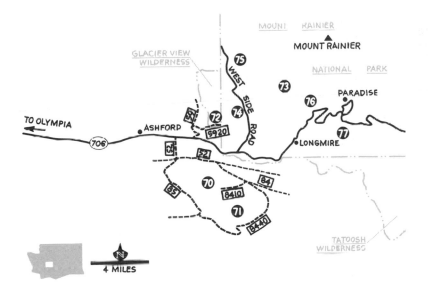

70. Bertha May and Granite Lakes

Type : Dayhike or backpack
Difficulty : Moderate–difficult for children
Hikable : July–October
One way : ¼ mile, ¾ mile, and 1½ miles
High point : 4175 feet
Elevation gain : 600 feet
Green Trails map : No. 301 Randle
U.S. Forest Service map : Gifford Pinchot

Three woodland lakes along a short forest trail are good choices for Scout groups, or families with young and inexperienced hikers. Children can swim in all three, but shorelines are soft and muddy in the first two.

Drive Highway 706 east from Ashford 3.4 miles towards Mount Rainier (Hike 73). Turn right on Kernahan Road, cross the Nisqually River, and in 1.5 miles turn left on road No. 52. At 5 miles from the highway go right on road No. 84. In 2 more miles turn right on No. 8410, signed "Teeley Creek Trail." Drive 3.9 miles to trail No. 251, elevation 3600 feet. Watch carefully as the trail is poorly signed.

An easy ¼ mile leads to Pothole Lake, a poor name for a lake large enough for several campsites, with a sizable outlet stream.

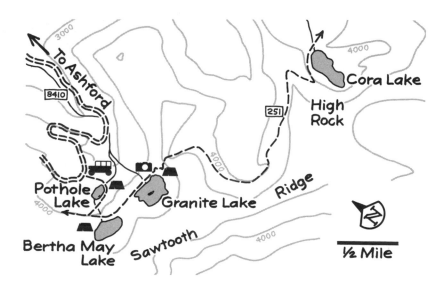

Fogbound Bertha May Lake

Climb steeply ½ mile through big old hemlocks to Bertha May Lake. Long and narrow, her shore lined with driftwood and blueberries, Bertha May has good campsites. Too bad that many hikers visiting this lake are beginners who aren't used to carrying out their own garbage.

In ½ mile more the trail climbs to the prettiest of the three, Granite Lake, elevation 4175 feet. Good campsites are near the outlet and scattered around the far side. Near the outlet are picture-window views of Mount Rainier.

High Rock Lookout and Mount Rainier

71. High Rock

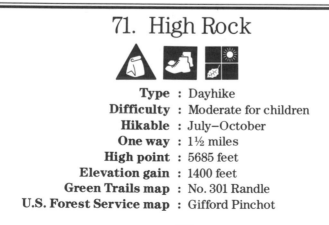

Type :	Dayhike
Difficulty :	Moderate for children
Hikable :	July–October
One way :	1½ miles
High point :	5685 feet
Elevation gain :	1400 feet
Green Trails map :	No. 301 Randle
U.S. Forest Service map :	Gifford Pinchot

One of the few lookouts still operating in the state, High Rock offers children a rare opportunity to talk with the fire lookout and see the Osborne fire-finder with which fires are located in minutes, then called in on the radio. This tiny perch is no place for a sleepwalker. The spectacular views of Mount Rainier and tiny Cora Lake 2000 feet below are like those from a small plane. Ask the lookout what it's like to be there in a storm — especially a lightning storm!

Drive Highway 706 3.4 miles east from Ashford towards Mount Rainier (Hike 73). Turn right on Kernahan Road, signed "Big Creek Campground-Packwood." Cross the Nisqually River on a narrow bridge and at 1.5 miles reach a junction. Go straight ahead on road No. 85, circling the south side of the Sawtooth Range. Turn left on road No. 8440 and at 11 miles total from the junction with road No. 52 reach the trailhead at Towhead Gap, elevation 4301 feet.

Trail No. 266, signed "High Rock," begins on the uphill side of the road and switchbacks steeply up through forest with occasional views of adjoining ridges. The last 200 yards are on steep solid rock into which handrails, painted for high visibility, have been set. At their end is the lookout, elevation 5685 feet.

The building is perched on the corner of a precipice. In a burrow directly below it lives a family of marmots. They come out to bask in the sun on their airy ledge and ponder the view of Mount Rainier. In early summer the young pups, much smaller than the adults, are extremely curious about hikers, especially the ones smaller than the adults.

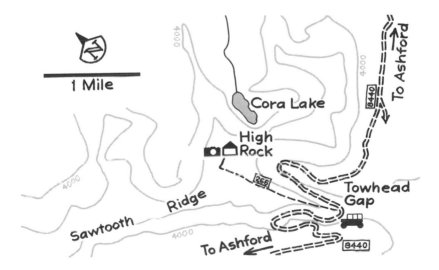

72. Lake Christine

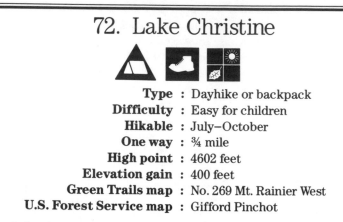

Type	:	Dayhike or backpack
Difficulty	:	Easy for children
Hikable	:	July–October
One way	:	¾ mile
High point	:	4602 feet
Elevation gain	:	400 feet
Green Trails map	:	No. 269 Mt. Rainier West
U.S. Forest Service map	:	Gifford Pinchot

A lovely little alpine lake in the Glacier View Wilderness offers campsites less than a mile from the road. The lake is too shallow for fish, but children will enjoy wading from logs and from the little peninsula on one shore.

Drive Highway 706 east from Ashford toward the Nisqually Entrance of Mount Rainier National Park (Hike 73). At 3.8 miles past

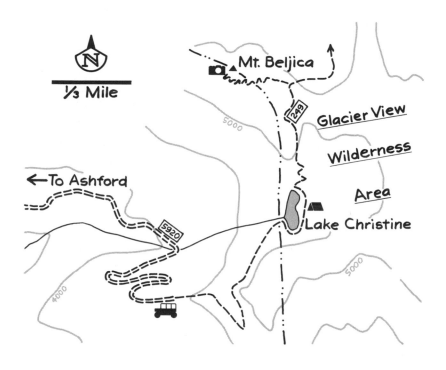

Ashford, turn left on Copper Creek road No. 59. Drive 5 miles, then turn right on No. 5920 and go another 2.4 miles to the trailhead, elevation 4400 feet.

Trail No. 249 starts very steeply, then moderates. Several portions have been sliced from a cliff; others are overhung by beetling cliffs. The ridges have been awesomely clearcut, and much of the remaining forest is by no means safe since only the last ⅛ mile is protected wilderness. At ¾ mile is Lake Christine, elevation 4802 feet.

Good camps are scattered on three sides of the lake, some with fireplace grills. An interesting day trip is a 1-mile ascent, gaining 700 feet, to the rounded rocky dome of Mount Beljica, elevation 5475 feet. To do this, proceed along the same trail beyond the lake to a saddle and turn left on the Mount Beljica trail; a very steep ½ mile takes you to the summit. Enjoy the views of Mount Adams, the remains of Mount St. Helens, and the Puyallup Glacier of Mount Rainier. Notice the lookout building on far-off Gobblers Knob. Mount Beljica itself was once a lookout point, but never had a building. Its unusual name is formed by the initials of the seven people who made the first ascent.

Mount Rainier, from Mount Beljica trail

Canada Jay and Mount Rainier, from Mirror Lake trail

73. Indian Henry's Hunting Ground

Type :	Dayhike
Difficulty :	Difficult for children
Hikable :	Mid-July–October
One way :	3½ miles
High point :	5400 feet
Elevation gain :	2100 feet
Green Trails map :	No. 269 Mt. Rainier West
National Park Service map :	Mount Rainier National Park Backcountry Trip Planner

The best-known mountain meadow on Mount Rainier's south side. See if it matches your conception of the Elysian Fields, the paradise of the ancient Greeks (also the name of another Rainier meadow, on the other side of the mountain). The trail is smooth and well graded, but what makes it memorable is a swinging suspension bridge high above Tahoma Creek at 2¼ miles. The bridge is at least 100 feet high so every parent should carefully supervise the crossing. Children like to run and jump on it to make it sway. (I do too.) Some hikers may not be at ease on the bridge; keep in mind that the sway can be minimized by walking slowly and putting each foot directly in the center.

The Nisqually Entrance to Mount Rainier National Park can be reached by way of Randle, Puyallup, or, from Tacoma, as described here. From I-5, take Exit 133 in Tacoma and follow Highway 7 east. The way is well marked. Pass Alder Lake and Elbe, and go straight ahead on Highway 706 another 15 miles through Ashford to the Nisqually Entrance of Mount Rainier National Park. In a scant 1 mile from the entrance, turn left on the West Side Road and go 4 miles to the Tahoma Creek trailhead, elevation 3200 feet.

The trail starts near what was once the Tahoma Creek Campground but no longer goes through it. It follows the creek — sometimes near the water, sometimes several hundred feet above it. This area has had a flood and mudslide from the Tahoma Glacier, cause unknown but not unspeculated on. A burst of volcanic steam beneath the ice? A change in the glacier's internal plumbing? Luckily no one was camped here at the time. In about 2 miles pass a small waterfall. At 2¼ miles join the Wonderland Trail, turning right. Cross Tahoma Creek on the suspension bridge and gaze upward at Glacier Island, between the Kautz and Tahoma glaciers. (As late as 1940 this *was* an island — the glaciers came around it on both sides.)

The trail now steepens. At 2½ miles step over a large root twisted like a giant python. As you climb, notice the forest changing from Douglas and silver fir to subalpine fir and from western hemlock to mountain hemlock. At 3¼ miles the flowers and heather begin; you emerge into open meadows with spectacular views of Mount Rainier at 5400 feet. (We counted over 20 species of flowers here.) The hike ends at 3½ miles, where you'll find the historic log guard station. For a side trip, at ¼ mile below the guard station take the Mirror Lakes trail, meandering ¾ mile to a small tarn with a big reflection.

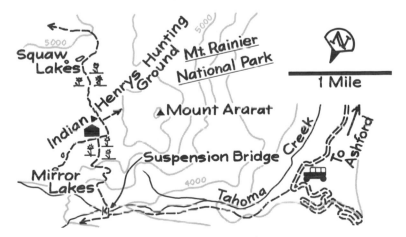

74. Lake George

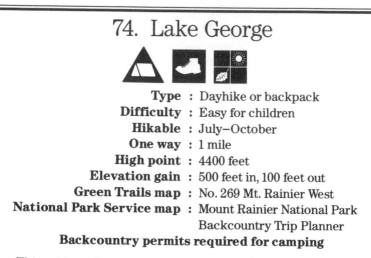

Type :	Dayhike or backpack
Difficulty :	Easy for children
Hikable :	July–October
One way :	1 mile
High point :	4400 feet
Elevation gain :	500 feet in, 100 feet out
Green Trails map :	No. 269 Mt. Rainier West
National Park Service map :	Mount Rainier National Park
	Backcountry Trip Planner

Backcountry permits required for camping

This wide trail passes through forest to a sparkling lake ideal for camping and swimming. Families may continue up to a lookout with a close-enough-to-touch view of the southwest side of Mount Rainier. The trail is wide and smooth as far as Lake George, but gains steadily to reach Gobblers Knob. Carry water and extra clothing, just in case it is windy on top.

From the Nisqually Entrance to Mount Rainier National Park (Hike 73), drive 1 mile and go left on the West Side Highway 7 miles to a large parking lot at Round Pass and the Lake George–Gobblers Knob trailhead, elevation 3900 feet.

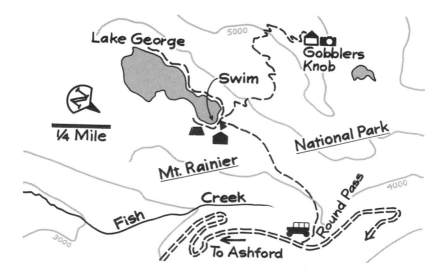

The trail begins on the level in big old trees, then tilts abruptly upward, gaining 300 feet in a scant ½ mile. Just as abruptly the angle slackens near a tree with a gaping hole and the remaining distance is an easy grade to a 4400-foot highpoint, then a drop to the shore of Lake George, elevation 4292 feet.

Campsites are to the left, but children will find the best swimming directly in front of the trail end. Whatever the day's plans, families will want to stop long enough to wade and splash. Both children and adults will enjoy peering at the tiny old log patrol cabin, and may want to take time to walk halfway around the lake and admire its mirroring of "The Mountain."

Older children (and their parents) will be attracted by the spectacular views from the lookout on Gobblers Knob, only 1½ steep miles and 1500 feet farther along the same trail. Begin the climb in forest. Eventually the trail reaches alpine rockeries where Rainier looms close, set off by clumps of paintbrush, heather, and penstemon. The friendly lookout always has time to talk to children and tell them about life on a lookout. Mine wanted to stay there and help.

Lake George

75. Klapatche Park

Type : Dayhike or backpack
Difficulty : Moderate for children
Hikable : Mid-July–October
One way : 2½ miles
High point : 5500 feet
Elevation gain : 1800 feet
Green Trails map : No. 269 Mt. Rainier West
National Park Service map : Mount Rainier National Park
Backcountry Trip Planner
Backcountry permits required for camping

This meadow-at-the-lake family camp is on the south side of Mount Rainier. The lake is small and warm, with spectacular views of Sunset Amphitheater. My children remember minnows and frogs in the lake, and deer in the meadows. The trail is fairly steep but wide and well groomed.

Drive 1 mile from the Nisqually Entrance of Mount Rainier National Park and turn left on the unpaved West Side Road (Hike 73). Cross St. Andrews Creek at 11 miles and park near the bridge, elevation 3700 feet.

From beyond the bridge, the trail climbs through old-growth forest, and switchbacks up to a ridge at 1½ miles where window views open to Rainier. At about 2 miles the way contours a wooded hill and with a few more switchbacks enters the meadowland of Klapatche Park, elevation 5500 feet.

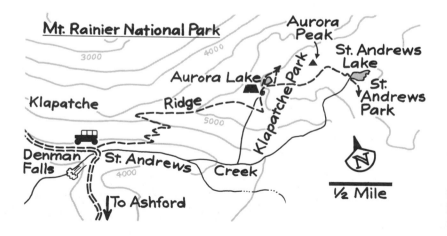

Because the lake nearly vanishes in late summer, do not rely on it for water. Campsites are few and a backcountry permit is required, so plan to arrive early enough at Longmire to obtain one.

After a night at the lake (and a beautiful sunrise) we climbed on the Wonderland Trail to lovely little St. Andrews Lake at 6000 feet, much more alpine in character than Klapatche. The children slid in snowbanks and whistled to marmots. Youngsters of greater size and ambition will want to explore the fairyland of rock buttresses, meltwater ponds, and surprising little flower gardens on the ridge leading to the glacier.

Aurora Lake, in Klapatche Park, and Mount Rainier

76. Comet Falls–Van Trump Park

Type	: Dayhike
Difficulty	: Difficult for children
Hikable	: Mid-July–October
One way to Comet Falls	: 2 miles
One way to Van Trump Park	: 3½ miles
High point	: 4900 feet
Elevation gain	: 1300 feet
Green Trails map	: No. 269 Mt. Rainier West
National Park Service map	: Mount Rainier National Park Backcountry Trip Planner

There are four good reasons to take this steep and rocky hike: (1) a spectacular waterfall, 320 frothing feet from brink to plunge basin, (2) alpine meadows, (3) Mount Rainier so close you can feel the glaciers' cold breath, and (4) frequent glimpses of deer and mountain goats. The trail is steep with some big steps, and in many places it is also rough and rocky. Even so, this hike beside a noisy creek is delightful.

From the Nisqually Entrance to Mount Rainier National Park (Hike 73) drive 10 miles toward Paradise to a small parking area signed "Van Trump Park" on the left side of the road. (If you reach the bridge over Christine Falls you have gone too far.) Elevation, 3600 feet.

The trail starts up from the left side of the parking area and is wide

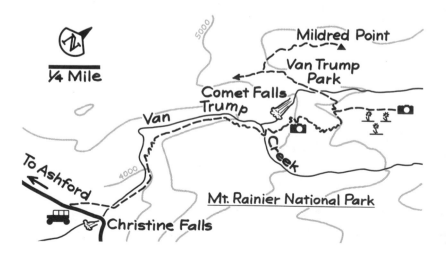

Comet Falls

and smooth as far as the bridge across Van Trump Creek. Stop on the bridge to look down into the rushing white water. Always within sound and often in sight of the creek, the trail climbs, sometimes steeply, over roots and boulders to the base of Comet Falls, elevation 4900 feet, at 2 miles. Sitting in the spray and mist and gazing upward at the falling water can be so fascinating that children (and adults) lose track of time. A favorite pastime is to pick out a spot of water as it runs over the brink, and follow it (with your eyes) until it blurs into the spray at the bottom.

It would be a shame to turn back here, so if you have enough energy, continue another steeply switchbacking mile (but on better trail) to Van Trump Park, where flower meadows extend into the very moraines of the Kautz Glacier, which tumbles from the summit ice cap. At 3 miles is a junction. Go right, climbing an exhausting staircase to a 5700-foot view-point amid flowers and subalpine trees.

Mount Rainier, from Pinnacle Peak saddle

77. Pinnacle Saddle

Type :	Dayhike
Difficulty :	Moderate for children
Hikable :	Mid-July–October
One way :	1½ miles
High point :	6000 feet
Elevation gain :	1200 feet
Green Trails map :	No. 270 Mt. Rainier East
National Park Service map :	Mount Rainier National Park
	Backcountry Trip Planner

A breathtakingly lovely view across valleys to the southern majesty of Mount Rainier is reached by a short but steep walk above Reflection Lakes. Wide and safe enough for small children, the trail switchbacks upward 1000 feet in 1¼ miles. Feast on the fat blueberries that line the trail in August and September.

From the Nisqually Entrance to Mount Rainier National Park, drive towards Paradise. Pass Longmire and Christine Falls, cross the Nisqually River, pass Narada Falls, and go right on the Stevens Canyon Road, signed "Ohanepecosh," to a parking area beside the first Reflection Lake. Stop to admire The Mountain's reflection, a good reason for the lake's name. A quick search here for tadpoles is mandatory. The Pinnacle Saddle trail starts on the opposite side of the road, elevation 4854 feet.

The smooth, well-maintained path crosses some snowpatches, which in early summer may stop the trip short. Mount Rainier stays behind your back, so you may want to turn around for frequent rest-stop views. At the saddle the trail is a shelf blasted out of Pinnacle's rocky shoulder. Hold children's hands here; the drop-off is abrupt. Turn around and gape. Above the lakes and Paradise are the moraines of Nisqually Glacier; follow the ice stream upward to the jutting buttress of Gibraltar Rock, and beyond that, the massive summit ice cap. At 1¼ miles and 6000 feet go through the saddle between Pinnacle and Plummer peaks for a whole new view of the South Cascades.

Climbers (and some in slippery shoes) often scramble up the hazardous cliffs to the top of Pinnacle Peak. This is not recommended for hikers and certainly not for children. Families will find plenty of satisfaction snacking amid the flowers.

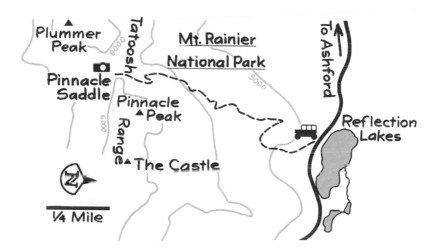

Caterpillar and friend

White Pass Highway

State Route 12

78. Packwood Lake...194
79. Grove of the Patriarchs...196
80. Shoe Lake...198
81. Deer Lake and Sand Lake...200

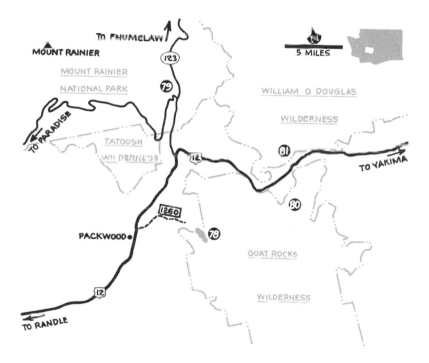

78. Packwood Lake

Type	: Dayhike or backpack
Difficulty	: Moderate for childn
Hikable	: June–November
One way	: 4½ miles
High point	: 2857 feet
Elevation gain	: 200 feet
Green Trails map	: No. 302 Packwood
U.S. Forest Service map	: Gifford Pinchot

One of the largest woodland lakes in the South Cascades is an easy stroll on a smooth, wide, and gentle trail. Camping, boating and fishing continue undisturbed on a shore beloved by families since early in the century.

All is not well, however. The outlet stream was dammed in 1963 for a power project. Although the permit states that the lake level is to be maintained, it is often lowered. But worst of all, the dam was built five feet higher than it needed to be, so there is always the possibility that the power-hungry utility will flood the lakeshore. To add insult to injury, motorcycles, three-wheelers, and four-wheelers are allowed on the power company's service road to the lakeshore. But there they stop. The lake itself is off-limits to them.

Drive Highway 12 south to the town of Packwood. At the upper end of town near the U.S. Forest Service ranger station, go right on the road signed Packwood Lake. Enter the Gifford Pinchot Forest at 0.9 mile and drive 6.2 miles to a large parking lot and the start of trail No. 78, elevation 2700 feet.

Packwood Lake and Johnson Peak

The trail starts in second growth forest, entering the Goat Rocks Wilderness at ¾ mile. Watch for spectacular views of Mount Rainier. At 1½ miles the old-growth forest begins. Children will be awed by these real-life giants, some at least 500 years old. Look too for groves of yew trees, whose bark is now being used in cancer research. Just before dropping to the lake, pass through an ancient rockslide that may have had a part in the creation of the lake by damming Lake Creek. At 4½ miles reach Packwood Lake, 2857 feet.

Two guard stations are at the lake, one of them a log structure built in 1910 and preserved as a historic landmark. A resort rents rowboats, rafts, and cabins in fishing season. A small store sells soup, sandwiches, and bait. The campground is just beyond the store. To escape the motorcyclists and their portable radios, Coleman lanterns, and beer, continue on to quieter campsites up the lake.

The partly glacier-fed lake, turquoise from the suspended rock flour, has a large wooded island in the center. Above rises 7487-foot Johnson Peak, where a band of mountain goats is headquartered. Named "Ackushnesh" by the Indians, the lake was renamed for Billy Packwood, who found it while prospecting with his son in the early 1900s. It was established as a Recreation Area in 1936 and as a Limited Area in 1946, but that status was removed in 1962 so the dam could be built.

Root system of large hemlock in Grove of the Patriarchs

79. Grove of the Patriarchs

Type	:	Dayhike
Difficulty	:	Easy for children
Hikable	:	May–November
One way	:	¼ mile
High point	:	2200 feet
Elevation gain	:	None
Green Trails map	:	No. 270 Mt. Rainier East
National Park Service map	:	Mount Rainier National Park Backcountry Trip Planner

The tremendous trees are bound to impress children — and grand-parents too — with their size, age, and venerable beauty. There are interpretive signs for parents, hollow trees for imaginative children to crawl inside, and a shallow creek for everyone to soak or splash in. A great spot to cool off on a hot day, and a big wide trail to hike on a rainy one.

Drive Highway 12 south through Packwood and continue about 8 miles toward White Pass. Go left at the junction with Highway 123, signed "Mount Rainier National Park." Enter the park and drive past the campground to a major junction; go left on the Stevens Canyon road signed "Paradise." Pass the entrance station and park on the far side of the Ohanepecosh River bridge. The trail starts beside the restroom.

The trail is mostly level. Look for the "squirrel overpass," a log suspended 10 feet over the trail like a freeway overpass. At a trail junction turn right and descend a short switchback to a suspension bridge that spans a shallow branch of the river to a loop trail. Go either way, winding through the Grove of the Patriarchs. There are 35 trees over 25 feet in diameter, some over 300 feet high, and all estimated to be between 800 to 1000 years old. Notice that some of the hemlocks are standing in midair on giant forklike roots. These trees were germinated and grown on nurse logs that long ago decayed and disappeared. Tell the children they provide homes for the seven dwarfs and other friendly woodland creatures.

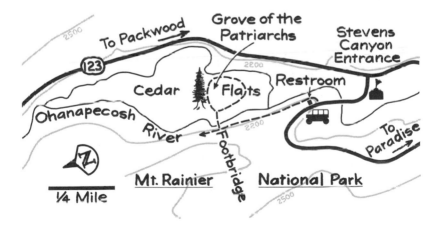

80. Shoe Lake

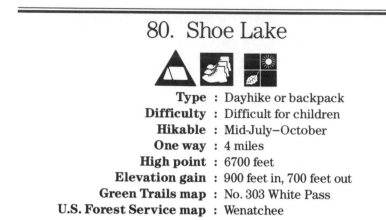

Type	: Dayhike or backpack
Difficulty	: Difficult for children
Hikable	: Mid-July–October
One way	: 4 miles
High point	: 6700 feet
Elevation gain	: 900 feet in, 700 feet out
Green Trails map	: No. 303 White Pass
U.S. Forest Service map	: Wenatchee

A thrilling ride up the White Pass chairlift — a pleasant way to gain 1500 feet of elevation while sitting down — can be combined with a walk along the Pacific Crest Trail through meadows, around a cirque, to the ridge overlooking Shoe Lake Basin. The lake itself is a fairly arduous destination for one day, so plan two or more days. (However, camping is not allowed at Shoe Lake; you'll have to continue another 1½ miles to Hidden Springs for a campsite.)

Drive Highway 12 to White Pass, elevation 4400 feet. If you plan to take the chairlift, park at the turnout for the White Pass Ski Area. If you plan to walk the entire distance, continue 0.8 mile east to where the Pacific Crest Trail crosses the highway. This alternative adds 3 more miles each way. Children will always vote for the chairlift: like adults, they would rather ride when there is no need to walk. Plus, the ride itself is spectacular.

From the top of the chairlift, 5961 feet, the trail drops 200 feet into a forest of subalpine fir. In ½ mile it joins the Pacific Crest Trail headed

Shoe Lake and snow-capped Goat Rocks

south. Enter the Goat Rocks Wilderness only briefly, then leave it again for a yet-to-be-constructed chairlift extension. The trail re-enters the Wilderness, climbing through meadows and around a large rocky cirque in the side of Hogback Mountain, above a meadow bench holding little Lake Miriam, which is not accessible by trail. Continue around the basin and up, surmounting a spur ridge at 6700 feet.

The view down to Shoe Lake should galvanize children to hurry down the switchbacks to the water's edge at 6200 feet. The view beyond to the snowfields, glaciers, and crags of Goat Rocks should also electrify most parents. Look for the two major peaks on the Cascade Crest — Old Snowy and Mount Gilbert. Red-yellow Tieton Peak is an eastward-jutting spur.

In the basin itself are fields of four-inch blueberry plants (the rest buried in ash), and indigo blue gentians. The lake is shallow, and swimmable on a warm day. I once saw a kingfisher skimming its surface. The encroaching small subalpine firs are explained by foresters as the product of a nine-year period of very dry winters between 1928 and 1937. This extended growing season meant that germination and establishment of the subalpine trees was more successful than usual. Fifty years later the little trees are filling in meadows where only flowers bloomed before.

If you want to stay overnight, good camps lie 1½ miles beyond at Hidden Springs.

81. Deer Lake and Sand Lake

Type	: Dayhike or backpack
Difficulty	: Easy for children
Hikable	: July–October
One way to Deer Lake	: 2½ miles
One way to Sand Lake	: 3½ miles
High point	: 5295 feet
Elevation gain	: 700 feet
Green Trails map	: No. 303 White Pass
U.S. Forest Service map	: Wenatchee

These two neat and tidy lakes lie along the Pacific Crest Trail in the William O. Douglas Wilderness. Deer Lake is deep and surrounded by forest. Sand Lake, the further, is bordered by meadows and tall trees but is so shallow that by midsummer finding usable water can be a problem.

Drive Highway 12 east to the summit of White Pass; 0.8 mile east of the pass is the Pacific Crest Trail crossing. Turn left and go 0.2 mile to the White Pass Campground and the hikers' parking area, elevation 4400 feet.

Start out north in forest on the Pacific Crest Trail; in summer this stretch is very dusty from horse traffic. At 1 mile enter the Douglas

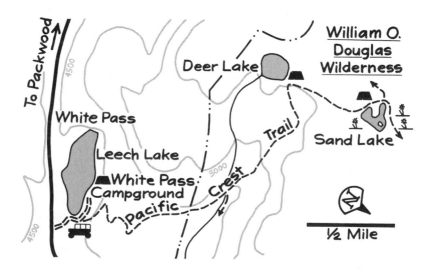

Wilderness. At 2½ miles a short side trail leads to Deer Lake, elevation 5206 feet, with good campsites and a sandy swimming beach.

Another scant 1 mile brings hikers to Sand Lake, elevation 5245 feet, and an interesting shoreline of alpine trees and flowers. A longtime hiker of these parts mused, after the most recent St. Helens blast, "I always *wondered* where all this sand came from." (St. Helens has been blowing "sand" for centuries.) Where the trail is cut into sidehills, exposing soil layers, you can see streaks of "sand" just like that now on the surface. Camping is just beyond the lake.

Pacific Crest Trail near Sand Lake

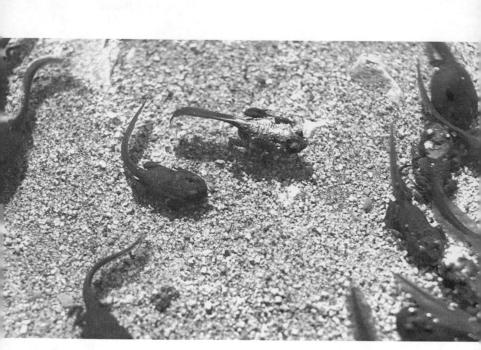

Polliwogs

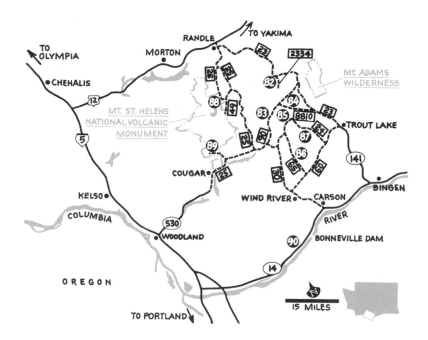

Southern Cascade Highways

State Routes 12, 503, 14, and 141

82. Council Bluff...204
83. Lewis River Trail...206
84. Sleeping Beauty...208
85. Steamboat Mountain...210
86. Thomas Lake...213
87. Indian Heaven Wilderness Vacation...214
88. Norway Pass...216
89. Butte Camp — Loowit Trail...218
90. Beacon Rock...220

Frog eggs just beginning to hatch

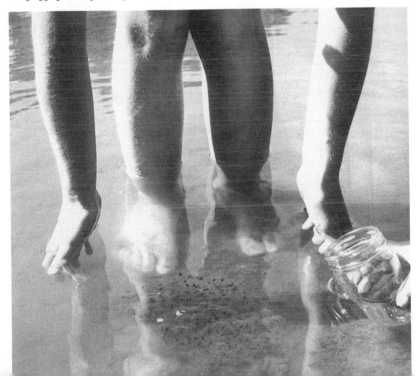

82. Council Bluff

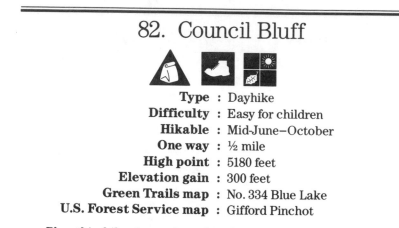

Type : Dayhike
Difficulty : Easy for children
Hikable : Mid-June–October
One way : ½ mile
High point : 5180 feet
Elevation gain : 300 feet
Green Trails map : No. 334 Blue Lake
U.S. Forest Service map : Gifford Pinchot

Plan this hike for a clear day. A very short climb through rock gardens leads to a spectacular viewpoint of Mounts Hood, Rainier, Adams, St. Helens — and Potato Hill too! If the Indians did not hold council meetings on this beauty spot, they should have.

Drive south from Randle on road No. 23 to Baby Shoe Pass and 1 mile beyond to a junction with road No. 2334. Turn right and go 1.9 miles to Council Lake Campground, where I once saw an honest-to-gosh tepee in one campsite. (Real tepees are sold by a number of outdoor outfitters, and they can't be beat for stand-up camping and for building wood fires *inside* your tent.) Drive through the campground and up a steep mile on

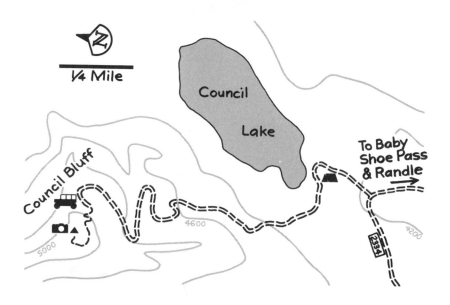

Mount Adams and Council Lake, from Council Bluff

a road barely passable for a family car. Ample turnaround and parking space at the top, elevation 4850 feet.

The ½-mile walk to the 5163-foot bluff carries hikers above surrounding ridges through clumps of flowers and juniper to knockout views of the Cascade volcanoes. Other landmarks in addition to those mentioned above are Steamboat Mountain, Sleeping Beauty, and Indian Heaven. Potato Hill? That is the wooded, cone-shaped hill to the north. It, too, is a volcano, now extinct. In fact, everything you see here is either a volcano or lava flow.

83. Lewis River Trail

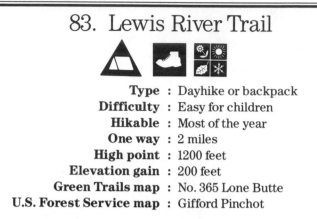

Type :	Dayhike or backpack
Difficulty :	Easy for children
Hikable :	Most of the year
One way :	2 miles
High point :	1200 feet
Elevation gain :	200 feet
Green Trails map :	No. 365 Lone Butte
U.S. Forest Service map :	Gifford Pinchot

The pride of the Gifford Pinchot National Forest is a gorgeous riverside walk among old-growth firs and cedars, past pools and rapids of the blue-green, glacier-fed Lewis River. Swimming, fishing, and camping are other assets. And the elevation is so low the trail is open all year.

The Lewis River Trail can be reached either from Randle, by going south on road No. 25, or, as described here, from Woodland. Leave I-5 at Woodland, Exit 21, and drive north on Highway 503. Beyond the town of Cougar, the highway becomes road No. 25. Shortly after passing the upper end of the Swift Reservoir, turn right on road No. 90 and drive 5.2 miles. Turn left on road No. 9039, go 1 mile, and park next to the Lewis River bridge, elevation 1000 feet.

Cross the bridge on foot and on the right find Lewis River trail No. 31. It begins in beautiful old-growth forest — fated to be just about the last preserved example of low-elevation big trees in this area. The way drops slightly, then levels to follow the river bank for ¾ mile. Nurse trees — downed logs sprouting new growth — give parents the chance to explain the birth-death-rebirth cycle of a forest left to nature's management. The trail moves from deep woods into second-growth deciduous trees and is bordered by oxalis, vanilla leaf, and heart-shaped leafed vancouveria, named for Captain George Vancouver, whose botanist, Archibald Menzies, found it in 1792. Briefly follow part of an old logging road; look for giant stumps from the *really* old growth, now gone. Visualize the logger of yesteryear balancing on narrow springboards inserted in the slots chopped in the sides. At about 1½ miles is a high point where you can see the crystal clear waters of Rush Creek gushing into the opaque green Lewis River. From here the trail follows the river

closely, passing moss-festooned maples and at 1¾ miles a good campsite near a deep pool.

Bolt Camp at 2 miles has a three-sided shelter built in the 1930s, still habitable in a rainstorm.

If time and energy permit, on returning to the car you can drive a
scant 1 mile back to road No. 9039 and walk the scant ½-mile trail to
Curly Creek viewpoint. On the opposite side of the river, Curly Creek
flows under a natural bridge and drops over a 60-foot waterfall directly
into the Lewis River.

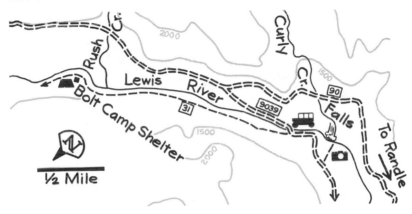

Old shelter at Bolt Camp on the Lewis River trail

Sleeping Beauty trail and Mount Adams

84. Sleeping Beauty

Type	: Dayhike
Difficulty	: Moderate for children
Hikable	: June–November
One way	: 1½ miles
High point	: 4907 feet
Elevation gain	: 1400 feet
Green Trails map	: No. 366 Mt. Adams West
U.S. Forest Service map	: Gifford Pinchot

The rocky profile of a lady, best seen from the town of Trout Lake, provides hikers with a trail that ascends to exciting views of Mount

Adams, Mount Hood, and the many little extinct volcanos of Indian Heaven. Children love looking for the beauty stretched out against the skyline, then scrambling upward on switchbacks to the summit.

Sleeping Beauty can be reached by driving south from Randle on roads No. 23 and No. 8810 or, as described here, from Trout Lake. Drive west from the Mount Adams Ranger Station 0.9 mile to road No. 88, turn right, and proceed north. At 5 miles turn right on road No. (8810)040 and go 7 miles, passing a spur road, to the trailhead, elevation 3500 feet.

Sleeping Beauty trail No. 37 begins on the south side of the peak. The way climbs steeply in an old forest of Douglas and grand firs. The wild flowers and undergrowth are typical of the dry side of the Cascades — buckbrush, pyrola, dogbane, pipsissewa, wild rose, and vancouveria. The trail follows the base of the peak for about 1¼ miles to the north side, leaving the woods to emerge onto exposed rock. From here the trail switchbacks up ¼ mile to the summit on tread blasted from the cliff. The steep side is banked up by a man-made rock wall; marvel at the hand labor it took to wedge tiny chips of stone vertically between larger rocks. At the summit it is hard to tell whether the highest point is the beauty's nose or chin. Local residents get into arguments about this important issue. Whichever, the trail ends at 4907 feet, on the lip of a cliff.

Old photographs show a lookout, built in 1931, surrounded by a sturdy fence. Both fence and building are gone now, so keep away from the cliff edge. In the lady's rock gardens, in season find glowing lavender and scarlet penstemon, arnica and valerian. Children will be exhilarated by the summit scramble and the feeling of being masters of all they survey.

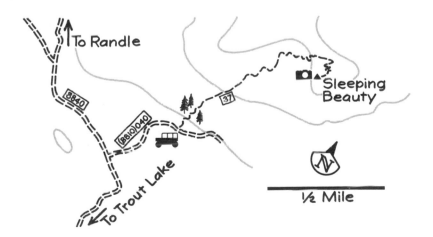

85. Steamboat Mountain

Type : Dayhike
Difficulty : Moderate for children
Hikable : June–October
One way : 1¼ miles
High point : 5424 feet
Elevation gain : 800 feet
Green Trails map : No. 366 Mt. Adams West
U.S. Forest Service map : Gifford Pinchot

The stunning view of four volcanos — Adams, St. Helens, Rainier, and Hood — makes clear why this was a lookout site from 1927 to 1971. Today it is part of a Research Natural Area set aside for scientific studies by forest ecologists. Children can enjoy the spooky character of the old subalpine trees as the trail winds up to a summit cliff; once there they can imagine being on the prow of a ship. Hang onto hands as you gaze down at three lakes, miles of forest, and out to four massive ice mountains.

Steamboat Mountain can be reached from Randle on road No. 23, Trout Lake on road No. 88, or from Carson on the Columbia River by way of roads No. 81 and No. 24. The logging roads are such a maze in this part of the Gifford Pinchot National Forest that the traveler is well-advised to obtain the Forest Service map, navigate to Mosquito Lakes near the junction of roads No. 24 and No. 8851, and find road No. 8854, signed

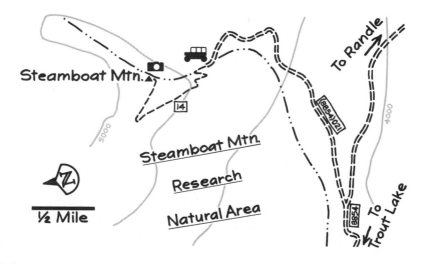

"Steamboat Lake." Drive 1 mile and go left, uphill, on road No. (8854)021 for another 1.4 miles to the road-end and parking lot in a gravel quarry, elevation 4700 feet.

Steamboat Mountain trail No. 14 is on the left side of the quarry. Before starting, look up at the awesome cliffs where the lookout once stood, and where you will soon stand. Fortunately the trail goes around the wooded backside.

The well-graded path is only a little over 1 mile long, but it's a very steep mile. Old subalpine firs with moss hanging from their branches create an especially spooky "guardian of the mountain" atmosphere. Just short of 1 mile the trail reaches the crest of the ridge. Go right along the ridge to the summit, elevation 5424 feet.

The east side of the broad summit is the edge of the cliff you saw from below. Look down to parked cars 800 feet below and out to spectacular views. We watched a raven that was level with us riding an updraft only 50 feet away. Keep a tight grip on small children here, lest they forget they don't have wings. **CAUTION**

Mosquito Lake, from Steamboat Mountain

Thomas Lake

86. Thomas Lake

Type	:	Dayhike or backpack
Difficulty	:	Easy for children
Hikable	:	July–October
One way	:	¾ mile
High point	:	4300 feet
Elevation gain	:	200 feet
Green Trails maps	:	No. 365 Lone Butte,
		No. 366 Mt. Adams West
U.S. Forest Service map	:	Gifford Pinchot

Take a short, easy trail to a cluster of five lakes, the most accessible in the Indian Heaven Wilderness. It's a great place to swim and catch fish, with any number of good campsites. (This would be an ideal hike to start a week-long vacation with small children, exploring the Indian Heaven Wilderness.) The trail is fine up to Thomas Lake, but beyond that the horse riders, traveling while the ground is still soft from melting snow, have turned the tread into quagmire. Once turned to mud, the trail isn't passable again for feet until after a month of dry weather.

By consulting the Forest Service map the trail can be reached from Randle, Trout Lake, or as described here from the town of Carson on Columbia River Highway 14. From Carson drive the Wind River Road to a junction at the end of the pavement near Milepost 30. Go right on road No. 30, signed "Lone Butte." At 1.7 miles from the junction go right on road No. 65 and at 6 miles from the junction find the Thomas Lake trailhead, elevation 4100 feet.

Thomas Lake trail No. 111 starts out in a clearcut, dotted in season with Indian paintbrush and lighted by the white torches of beargrass. At ½ mile the way enters the Indian Heaven Wilderness. At ¾ mile is a campsite between three lakes: Dee and Heather on the left, Thomas on the right. A few hundred feet beyond Thomas Lake is a junction; keep left to reach Eunice Lake. Lake Kwaddis is reached by a way trail around Thomas Lake. All the lakes are at about 4300 feet.

If you decide to explore the center of the Indian Heaven lakes country, head toward Eunice Lake and go right at the junction. The path gains 150 feet, then levels off and passes marshy meadows, shallow Brader Lake, and the quagmire left by horses. Children will be enchanted as forest becomes intermingled with parklike meadows dappled with ponds, pools, and lakelets.

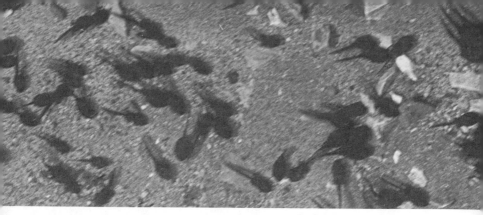

Polliwogs

87. Indian Heaven Wilderness Vacation

Type	:	Dayhike or backpack
Difficulty	:	Moderate for children
Hikable	:	July–October
One way to Cultus Lake	:	2 miles
Loop trip	:	15 miles
High point	:	5300 feet
Elevation gain	:	1800 feet
Green Trails maps	:	No. 365 Lone Butte,
		No. 366 Mt. Adams West
U.S. Forest Service map	:	Gifford Pinchot

Surrounded by a giant tree farm, Indian Heaven is a wild oasis, with 38 miles of trail through forest intermingled with parklike meadows, over 30 named lakes, and 100 or more nameless tarns. In my opinion, Indian Heaven is one of the three best places in the state to take young children on a week-long backpack. There are nine trails leading into the long, narrow wilderness. The one recommended here is from Cultus Creek Campground.

Cultus Creek Campground can be reached from Randle on road No. 23, from Trout Lake on roads No. 88 and No. 24, or from Wind River as described here. Whichever route is chosen, a Gifford Pinchot National Forest map is *essential* to figure out the maze of roads.

From Carson on the Columbia River, drive north on the Wind River Road to a junction near milepost 30. Turn right on road No. 30, signed "Lone Butte," and drive to road No. 24. Go right, passing the Indian Berry Fields, to Cultus Creek Campground, and park near the entrance, elevation 3958 feet.

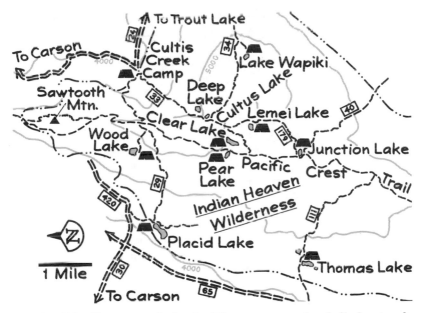

Trail No. 33 starts at the back of the campground and climbs steeply through forest (it gains 700 feet in the first mile), to a good view of Mount Adams. Thereafter the trail is more moderate, climbing 400 feet in the second mile to Cultus Lake and campsites near the outlet, 5150 feet.

Among the day trips from Cultus Lake is Deep Lake, a short distance away; the trail is near the outlet stream. For another side trip, continue on trail No. 33 for ¼ mile, then turn onto trail No. 34 and climb to a 5600-foot viewpoint on the side of Lemie Rock.

The most fun is a lazy two- to four-day loop from Cultus Lake. Stay on trail No. 33, climbing over a 5300-foot pass. In a scant mile go left on trail No. 179 and camp near Lemie Lake, elevation 4800 feet. Then move on 1 mile to campsites at Junction Lake, elevation 4700 feet, at the junction of trail No. 33 and the Pacific Crest Trail. From there take a 2¼-mile side trip (each way) on the Pacific Crest Trail to Blue Lake. From Junction Lake you can also join the Pacific Crest Trail and hike north 1 mile to Bear Lake, elevation 4700 feet. Camp here and with the help of a map find Elk, Deer, and Clear lakes. Then return to Cultus Creek Campground.

The entire loop can be hiked in a long day. But don't. Take time to do all the important things — wading and swimming in the lakes, searching for tadpoles in ponds and frogs in the meadows. Because snowpatches linger into August at this altitude, on a hot day snowball fights are inevitable. Just one precaution: all those lakes and ponds mean hordes of mosquitoes, so be prepared. But once in Indian Heaven, no child will ever want to leave.

88. Norway Pass

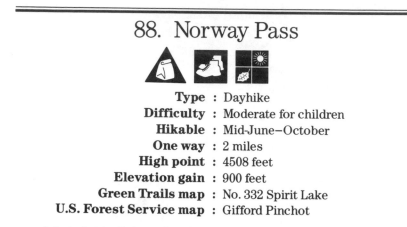

Type :	Dayhike
Difficulty :	Moderate for children
Hikable :	Mid-June–October
One way :	2 miles
High point :	4508 feet
Elevation gain :	900 feet
Green Trails map :	No. 332 Spirit Lake
U.S. Forest Service map :	Gifford Pinchot

A hot, dry trail through a desolation of timber downed by the 1980 blast of Mount St. Helens leads to one of the most spectacular viewpoints of the disaster area. You can look across Spirit Lake to the crater and smoldering dome. One-third of the lake is still covered by driftwood blown in by the eruption and washed into the lake in the ensuing tidal wave. On the lakeshore below Norway Pass, the giant wave swept everything bare for 500 feet up the hillside. Notice how the trees facing the mountain are lying flat in a straight line from the crater, while behind the ridge the trees are crisscrossed as the turbulent wave of supersonic air eddied behind the ridge tops. Be sure to carry plenty of drinking

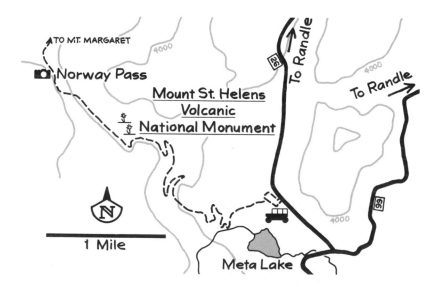

water, available at the trailhead rest rooms — all shade trees have been flattened.

Drive road No. 25 either 22 miles south from Randle or 44 miles north from Cougar, and turn uphill on road No. 99, signed Mount St. Helens–Windy Ridge Viewpoint. At 8.9 miles from the junction turn right on Ryan Lake road No. 26, and in 1 mile reach Norway Pass trailhead, elevation 3600 feet.

The trail starts at the far end of the parking lot, first meandering a bit through fallen timber and silvery snags, then starting a long series of switchbacks above Meta Lake. At about 1¼ miles the trail rounds a shoulder, drops a bit, and levels off. At 2 miles is Norway Pass, elevation 4508 feet, and the view.

Everywhere new beginnings of life are springing up: fireweed, berries, and little firs. For some reason the avalanche lilies on this hill flower with six or seven blossoms to a stem, unlike the usual pattern of two to three. The trail continues up Mount Margaret, but the views of the lake are no better.

Norway Pass, log-covered Spirit Lake, and Mount St. Helens

89. Butte Camp–Loowit Trail

Type	: Dayhike or backpack
Difficulty	: Difficult for children
Hikable	: June–October
One way	: 3½ miles
High point	: 4600 feet
Elevation gain	: 1500 feet
Green Trails map	: No. 364S Mt. St. Helens
U.S. Forest Service map	: Gifford Pinchot

The steep trail climbs to rock gardens where summit climbers on the south side of Mount St. Helens begin their ascent. Children will be interested in seeing climbers in their clinking, gaudy costumes, and may look forward to being old enough to make the climb themselves someday. (When they are ready, they'll learn that the Big Blast downgraded St. Helens to a mere hike.) A small mudflow below the trail and quantities of ash are mementos of the 1980 eruption.

With the aid of the Forest Service map the Butte Camp trailhead can be reached from Randle on road No. 23 or as described here from the Woodland exit on I-5. At Woodland go north on State Highway 503, which past the town of Cougar becomes road No. 90. At 6.8 miles from Cougar go left on road No. 81. At 10 miles is a small parking area and trail No. 238, signed "Butte Camp and Loowit Trail," elevation 3100 feet.

The trail begins in subalpine forest, makes a short switchback, crosses an ancient lava flow, an old clearcut, and in ½ mile reaches a junction. Go right on trail No. 238A, signed "Butte Camp and Loowit Trail." ("Loowit" is the Indian name for the woman who became Mount St. Helens.) This trail enters old-growth forest and, with some downs but more ups, arrives in 2½ miles at Butte camp, elevation 4000 feet. There are level campsites and water. Views extend to Mount Adams and the country between the two volcanoes.

From the camp the trail climbs steeply to meadows, levels, then tips up again to end at timberline, elevation 4600 feet, 3½ miles from the road.

Above here climbers ascend pumice slopes and snow. Hiking families will be satisfied with views south to Mount Hood and Mount Jefferson, east to Mount Adams and other peaks of the Cascades, and discussion of the wealth of forms of volcanic activity around them.

Trail to Butte Camp

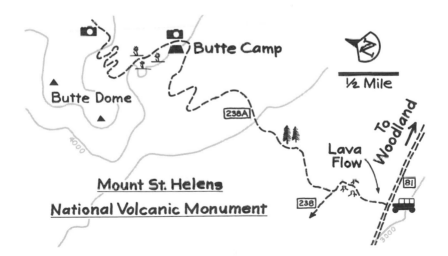

90. Beacon Rock

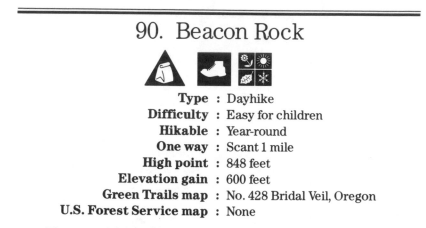

Type	: Dayhike
Difficulty	: Easy for children
Hikable	: Year-round
One way	: Scant 1 mile
High point	: 848 feet
Elevation gain	: 600 feet
Green Trails map	: No. 428 Bridal Veil, Oregon
U.S. Forest Service map	: None

The most famous rock in the Columbia Gorge makes a short and exciting hike for children, safe enough if they understand the hazards of stepping off the railed pathways. In 1915, Henry Biddle, its original owner, began building the trail, some of which still bears the marks of his blasting. The rock was not set aside as a Washington State Park until Biddle, who had offered it to Washington and been refused, offered it to Oregon, which was eager to get it. At that point Washington also became eager and accepted it. The views extend east to Bonneville Dam, west to Crown Point, and down to freight trains, boats, barges, and cars.

From I-5 at Vancouver drive east 34.5 miles on Highway 14, along the Columbia River, to the base of the towering rock and a large parking lot and rest room, elevation 250 feet.

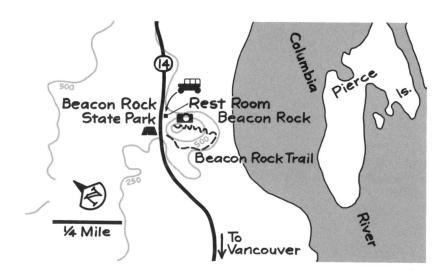

Beacon Rock trail.

The trail, wide enough to walk two abreast, begins on the west side of the parking lot. Circle the rock to the river side where the switchbacks start up. Children are in no danger if they stay on the trail, but if the handrails are too high for short arms, parents may choose to hold hands instead. The way zigzags steeply upward. Wooden catwalks bridge cracks in the rock and, much to the children's delight, the trail itself, a switchback below.

Views from the top are as exhilarating as those from the wing of an airplane. Gaze down on Bonneville Dam, across the river to Nesmith Point, northeast to Hamilton Mountain, and at all the trains and ships below.

Hoh River Rain Forest

Olympic Peninsula Highway

U.S. 101

91. Skokomish River...224

92. Lower Lena Lake...226

93. Hurricane Hill...228

94. Humes Ranch...230

95. Olympic Hot Springs...232

96. Soleduck Falls — Deer Lake...234

97. Second Beach and Third Beach...236

98. Hoh River Rain Forest...238

99. South Fork Hoh River...240

100. Dungeness Spit...242

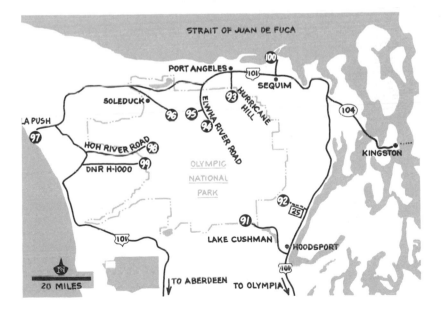

91. Skokomish River

Type : Dayhike
Difficulty : Easy for children
Hikable : May–November
Loop trip : 2 miles
High point : 1000 feet
Elevation gain : 200 feet
Green Trails map : No. 167 Mount Steel
Map : Olympic National Forest/
Olympic National Park

Walking this magical river loop in Olympic National Park can be done in an hour. However, with small children the possibilities for play along the way are infinite. Enormous trees with trunks set on stilt-like roots border river pools and rapids, calling to waders and paddlers. In fact, an hour is not enough. Better allow half a day.

Drive U.S. 101 along Hood Canal to Hoodsport. Turn uphill (west) on the Lake Cushman road, curving around Lake Cushman to the Staircase Ranger Station, elevation 785 feet. Look for a sign labeled "Staircase Rapids Trail" and another explaining that it goes along part of the route of the 1890 O'Neil Expedition.

Begin by crossing the North Fork Skokomish River on a gated bridge. Pass a park housing area and follow the level O'Neil Pass trail

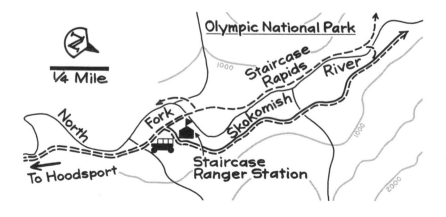

Footbridge across the North Fork Skokomish River

through deep forest by the Skokomish River. Pools and rapids are bordered by very old trees. Before this area became part of the park there was some selective logging, but most of the remaining trees are at least 250 years old. Take time to admire the Big Cedar, ¼ mile to the left. It is 43 feet in circumference at the base. At the Red Reef look for a deep pool beside a large red rock — a great place to swim. Beyond, are a cedar with a root like an arm buried to the elbow, Dolly Pool, and the Staircase Rapids.

At ¾ mile the trail divides. Go right past an enormous boulder overhanging the trail like half of a cave roof. Cross the river on an arched bridge, climb a few feet, and go right ending the loop on an old road built in the 1930s. When the early summer flooding is over, there are many more pools and gravel bars to swim and play on.

92. Lower Lena Lake

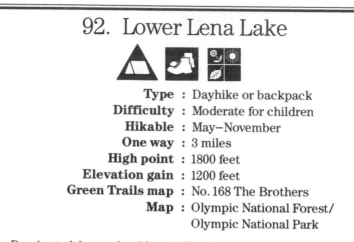

Type :	Dayhike or backpack
Difficulty :	Moderate for children
Hikable :	May–November
One way :	3 miles
High point :	1800 feet
Elevation gain :	1200 feet
Green Trails map :	No. 168 The Brothers
Map :	Olympic National Forest/
	Olympic National Park

Dominated by a shoulder of The Brothers, this forest lake was formed thousands of years ago by a massive rockslide that dammed the

Lena Lake

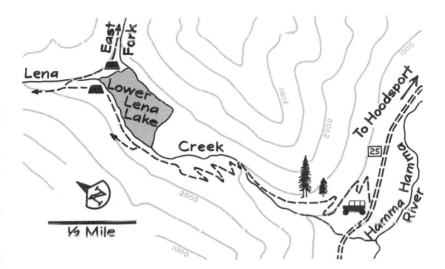

valley. The "dam" leaks and the lake resembles a reservoir in that the water rises and falls with the season. Wading and swimming are possible, but even in summer the water is so cold that only a child will enjoy it. This is one of the most popular hikes on the eastern slope of the Olympic Mountains, so the trail is eroded by the thousands of feet that have traveled it. Expect many roots and rocks for little feet to tumble over.

Lower Lena Lake has no protection. While Upper Lena Lake is in Olympic National Park, and The Brothers is in The Brothers Wilderness, a hydroelectric proposal has Lower Lena Lake facing a possible road and logging.

Drive U.S. 101 on Hood Canal to a mile north of the Hamma Hamma River bridge. Go uphill on Hamma Hamma River road No. 25. At 9.5 miles from the highway reach the Lena Lake trailhead, elevation 685 feet.

The trail switchbacks through an area that was first logged (by railroad) in 1931. The half-century-old trees look pretty good-sized until, at approximately ¾ mile, the trail enters old-growth forest — the *really* big trees. At 1½ miles the way crosses a dry streambed of Lena Creek, which runs underground most of the year. If time permits, explore the caves made by giant boulders lying on top of nature's dam, and marvel at the size of the trees growing on it. That rockslide was a long time ago! At 3 miles reach the shore and outlet of Lower Lena Lake, 1800 feet.

For camping, follow the trail around the lakeshore. When the lake is full, there will be a 150-foot climb over a rock buttress. At 3½ miles, at the inlet, are the best campsites, some of which have substantial fireplaces and even barbecues. Point out to children the scar on the hillside across the lake where the landslide came from.

Deer near Hurricane Ridge Visitors Center

93. Hurricane Hill

Type :	Dayhike
Difficulty :	Easy for children
Hikable :	Late July–October
One way :	1¼ miles
High point :	5757 feet
Elevation gain :	700 feet
Green Trails map :	No. 134 Mt. Olympus
Map :	Olympic National Forest/ Olympic National Park

A stroll through flower fields on a gently graded asphalt path to the site of a former Forest Service lookout enables families to gaze at 360 degrees of glorious views. To the south lie the great chasm of the Elwha River and the peaks of the central Olympics. Below is Port Angeles, the Strait of Juan de Fuca, and on beyond, Vancouver Island. If the day is cloudless, look east for the San Juans and Mount Baker.

From Port Angeles follow signs to the Hurricane Ridge road, pass the Olympic National Park's Visitors Center, and enter the park. Pass the Hurricane Ridge Visitors Center at 18 miles, and continue to the road end, elevation 5000 feet.

Follow the asphalt path 1¼ miles, gaining 700 feet, to the top of the hill. The meadows are dappled with clumps of subalpine fir and carpeted with lupine, valerian, penstemon, and paintbrush.

94. Humes Ranch

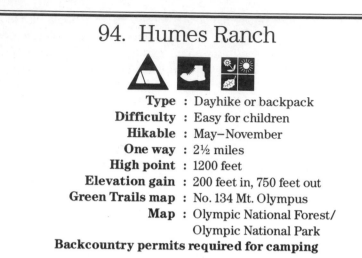

Type : Dayhike or backpack
Difficulty : Easy for children
Hikable : May–November
One way : 2½ miles
High point : 1200 feet
Elevation gain : 200 feet in, 750 feet out
Green Trails map : No. 134 Mt. Olympus
Map : Olympic National Forest/
Olympic National Park
Backcountry permits required for camping

See wildlife and learn a bit of Olympic history on this popular Elwha River trail. Although it makes a good dayhike for children, it is even better as an overnight backpack, with more opportunities to see deer and elk.

Drive U.S. 101 west from Port Angeles 8 miles and turn left on the Elwha River road. In 4 miles, just beyond the Elwha ranger station (backpackers get overnight permits here), turn left again on a dirt road signed "Whiskey Bend" and continue for another 4.3 miles. At the end

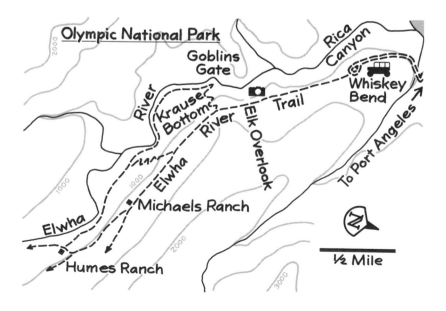

Humes Ranch

of the steep, narrow road find a parking lot and trailhead, elevation 1200 feet.

The trail begins in forest grown up since a fire in the early 1900s. At ¾ mile a side trail descends several hundred feet to Elk Overlook and an aerial view of the Elwha River. You can look down on the former pasture of a pioneer homesteader, Bill Anderson, that still attracts grazing deer and elk.

At approximately 1 mile the trail reaches its highest point and starts descending through the blackened stumps of a 1977 fire. At 1½ miles pass a side trail to Krause Bottom and in another ½ mile reach Michaels Ranch cabin, dating from 1906 and now a historic site. A few hundred feet beyond the cabin go right on the Dodger Point — Humes Ranch trail. At the next junction stay right, losing 250 feet in the final ½ mile to the Humes Ranch.

The pasture was cleared, the half-dozen fruit trees planted, and the cabin built in 1900 by two brothers, Grant and Will Humes. Imagine what it must have been like to live here then, 14 miles from the nearest road. Farm machinery and supplies had to be packed in by horse or on the farmer's back. Why are the pastures the pioneers created still open fields, unlike more recent clearings that are soon overgrown? Do grazing elk and deer play a part?

For camping, find the trail on the river side of the pasture and drop another 100 feet to the river. Watch for deer and elk grazing at dusk and dawn. To return, follow the lower trail from Humes Ranch, signed "Krause Bottom," and with numerous switchbacks return to the Elwha River trail near the Michaels Ranch cabin.

95. Olympic Hot Springs

Type : Dayhike or backpack
Difficulty : Easy for children
Hikable : June–November
One way : 2½ miles
High point : 2061 feet
Elevation gain : 300 feet
Green Trails map : No. 134 Mt. Olympus
Map : Olympic National Forest/
Olympic National Park
Backcountry permits required for camping

Soaking in small natural hot tubs set in Olympic National Park forest is a delight at any age, but families can enjoy the experience together at Olympic Hot Springs. A road walk of 2½ miles is the prerequisite; a large campground remains from the days when access by car was possible. Before that the area was a popular resort built in the 1920s, an era when "taking the waters" at a hot mineral spring was an American passion. Families still make a weekend of it here, soaking by night or day.

Drive U.S. 101 west from Port Angeles and turn left on the Elwha River road. Pass the Elwha Ranger Station (backpackers get overnight permits here), then Lake Mills. Ten miles from the highway reach the parking area, where the road is gated. Elevation, 1750 feet.

The old road, shaded by tall trees, crosses a creek in the first ¼

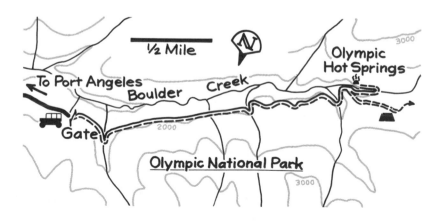

mile. It is occasionally used by Park Service vehicles, but usually hikers encounter only other hikers. Children can hold parents' hands and walk abreast. The mineral-scented steam drifting down the road alerts families to their destination, elevation 2061 feet.

For camping, go right. For the hot springs, cross a bridge over Boulder Creek. The nearby sign reveals that the minerals present in highest percentage are sodium and silica, which give the alkaline water a pH rating of 9.5. Children will be interested in the descriptive sign showing how surface water drops through rocks down to the earth's core, where it is superheated, then forced upward to form the hot springs.

Along the wooded path are at least seven pools to sample, ranging in temperature from lukewarm to 187 degrees! Most of the shallow, rock-lined pools are too small for more than two or three people. Two larger pools close together offer a family the opportunity to simmer in one, then cool off in the other. Take your choice of temperatures and degree of seclusion. Depending on the other bathers, there may be some legitimate concern over water pollution; expect to encounter some skinny-dipping too.

A warm pool at Olympic Hot Springs

96. Soleduck Falls–Deer Lake

Type	:	Dayhike or backpack
Difficulty	:	Easy for children
Hikable	:	June–October
One way to Soleduck Falls	:	1 mile
One way to Deer Lake	:	4 miles
High point	:	2000 feet and 3500 feet
Elevation gain	:	None to falls
		1500 feet to Deer Lake
Green Trails map	:	No. 133 Mt. Tom
Map	:	Olympic National Forest/
		Olympic National Park

This hike takes you through an old-growth forest with a green shag rug covering of moss and flowers to a thundering waterfall in a deep gorge. If the children are willing, climb to campsites near a subalpine lake.

Drive U.S. 101 west 2 miles from Lake Crescent, and turn left on the Soleduck River road. Drive 14.2 miles, passing Soleduck Hot Springs resort, and continue to the road end parking lot, elevation 2000 feet.

With minor ups and downs, the broad smooth trail travels through a magnificent stand of old-growth fir, hemlock, and an occasional Sitka spruce. In 1 mile reach a junction and shelter with many campsites and a good view of the falls from the trail bridge, elevation 2000 feet. Children

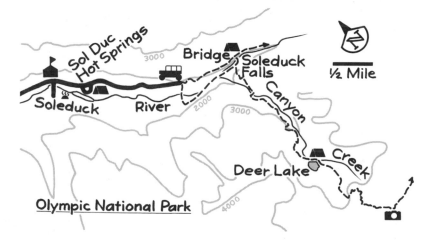

Soleduck Falls

should be carefully supervised here, because below the falls is a deep
canyon.

To continue on to Deer Lake, cross the Soleduck River on the bridge, wet with the spray from Soleduck Falls. Children will enjoy standing here in the spray, watching the water drop. Beyond this point the trail steepens in earnest. At 2 miles you cross Canyon Creek, and at 4 miles reach Deer Lake and the campsites, elevation 3500 feet. Spend a day here and wander up through heather and flower fields to High Divide, with its dramatic views across the Hoh Valley to the glaciers on Mount Olympus.

97. Second Beach and Third Beach

Type	: Dayhike or backpack
Difficulty	: Easy for children
Hikable	: Year-round
One way to Second Beach	: ¾ mile
One way to Third Beach	: 1⅓ miles
High point	: 300 feet
Elevation loss	: 100 feet and 300 feet
Green Trails map	: No. 163S La Push
Map	: Olympic National Forest/ Olympic National Park

Backcountry permits required for camping

The most accessible of the truly "wilderness ocean" beaches of Olympic National Park's Pacific Ocean Section, prosaically named Second Beach and Third Beach, lie immediately south of First Beach, at the Quilleute village of La Push. They are wide and sandy at low tide, with spectacular offshore islands and sea stacks, surf, and beachside camping. Either beach can be a paradise on a warm day, but the same attractions can be enjoyed even in the long, gray months of winter.

Drive U.S. 101 exactly 1 mile north of Forks, and turn west on the La Push–Mora road. Drive 7.9 miles to a junction. Take the left fork toward La Push. (The right fork goes to Mora Campground and Rialto Beach.) At 3.9 miles from the junction is the Third Beach trailhead, elevation 300 feet, and at 5.3 miles, only 0.8 mile short of La Push, is the Second Beach trailhead, elevation 100 feet.

The mostly level 1⅓-mile trail to Third Beach travels through old forest, then abruptly plunges off the plateau in a series of switchbacks

before arriving at the long, curving beach of Strawberry Bay. Campsites in the creek ravine at the trail end are protected from the wind unless it comes from the west (which it usually does). On both trails, getting across the wide belt of slippery driftwood onto open beach can be **CAUTION** difficult and dangerous.

Walk the beach ½ mile south for a closer view of the waterfall plummeting down the sea cliffs of Taylor Point into the surf. Backpackers take the trail over Taylor Point to begin a 20-mile wilderness beach walk to the mouth of the Hoh River.

The ¾-mile trail to Second Beach is shorter and the beach is wide, sandy, and has more spectacular sea stacks and offshore islands. The last ¼ mile of the trail is down a wooden staircase to the shoreline. Campsites are very limited but they can be found here and there on tiny benches above the high tide. (In the good weather of summer, during moderate tides, it is safe to camp on certain of the higher parts of both beaches.) Boil all water at both beaches.

Both beaches offer wonderful play possibilities: exploring tide pools, climbing giant driftwood logs, running in the surf. The temperature is the same winter and summer — bitingly cold. Whales are often observed from February to May, and throughout the year eagles perch on snags. Bring a kite — there's always plenty of wind, and it drives the gulls crazy. Wear boots for walking around slippery rocks near the tide pools. Camping near the ocean can be memorable on a windless night. Or a stormy one.

Sea stack at Second Beach

Hoh River Rain Forest

98. Hoh River Rain Forest

Type :	Dayhike or backpack
Difficulty :	Easy for children
Hikable :	Most of the year
One way :	3 miles
High point :	700 feet
Elevation gain :	120 feet
Green Trails map :	No. 133 Mt. Tom
Map :	Olympic National Forest/
	Olympic National Park

Backcountry permits required for camping

The world-famous rain forest is accessible most of the year. Children will love seeing the huge Roosevelt elk, which through their browsing and grazing keep the forest floor cropped of undergrowth and looking parklike. The chances of seeing them are best in late fall and winter, when herds are down in the valley and most tourists are gone, but one resident band can be seen even in busy summer months. The Hoh River trail extends 17 miles, all the way to the edge of the Blue Glacier on Mount Olympus; however, families can amply savor the beauty of the rain forest in the 3 miles to the Mount Tom Creek trail junction.

Drive Highway 101 north from Aberdeen or south from Forks and turn east on the Hoh River road. Drive 19 miles to the Hoh Visitors Center, elevation 578 feet.

Begin at the Visitors Center on a paved trail that turns to gravel, then soil. Hikers pass through old-growth Sitka spruce and Douglas fir interspersed with bigleaf maple, all festooned with club moss and feathered with licorice fern. Elk have cropped the forest floor plants they find tasty, leaving a green carpet of ferns, moss and oxalis. The most likely times and places to see the big animals, silently moving together, are early in the morning on the grassy terraces and gravel bars. One October morning when I was there, a large bull was moving his 20 cows across the terrace and through the river. A long strand of moss was draped rakishly across one horn. He bugled a challenge at me to make it clear they were *his* cows and I couldn't have them.

At 3 miles reach the Mount Tom Creek trail and follow it to the bank of the Hoh River, elevation 700 feet. The river's grassy terrace offers excellent tent sites, but build campfires on the gravel bar, not in the meadow. Children can play in the backwater pools.

Happy Four, at 6 miles from the Visitors Center, is an excellent destination for a second day. The old shelter there is highly appreciated during the rain spells, which provide the valley with 150 inches of rain a year.

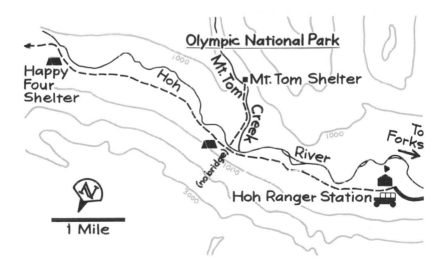

99. South Fork Hoh River

Type : Dayhike or backpack
Difficulty : Moderate for children
Hikable : April–November
One way : 2½ miles
High point : 800 feet
Elevation gain : 120 feet
Green Trails map : No. 133 Mt. Tom
Map : Olympic National Forest/
Olympic National Park
Backcountry permits required for camping

A gentle trail on river terraces leads into a uniquely beautiful old-growth rain forest. Children will be bemused to learn that the grazing of the elk maintains the open, parklike quality of this place; with luck they may see some of the band. Another attraction is the chance for solitude — away from the crowds on the Hoh Rain Forest trail. While this trail has very little elevation gain, there are several ups and downs. About two-thirds is smooth and easy going, but the remainder is rough and toddlers will need help. For this reason, the trail is classed as moderate.

Drive U.S. 101 from either Kalaloch or Forks to 0.6 mile south of the Hoh River bridge, near signpost 176. Turn south onto the Clearwater Corrections Center Road. At 6.7 miles turn left and follow road No. H-1000, passing numerous side roads. (Watch carefully. Some may look like the main road.) At 7.4 miles, cross the South Fork Hoh River on a concrete bridge, pass the S.F. (South Fork) Hoh Campground and drive 2.8 miles more to the road end and trailhead, elevation 700 feet.

The trail begins by dropping briefly on rocky tread to a stand of young Sitka spruce. If the children clutch a handful of their bristly needles, they will see why elk prefer dining on young hemlocks instead. (Paradoxically, the favorite elk "salad" is devil's club, which should not make for a smooth swallow either!). At ¼ mile enter Olympic National Park and at ¾ mile look for the first of the enormous old-growth firs on the right, or downhill, side of the trail. Its diameter is 9 feet, 8½ inches; its age at least 500 years. From here on many 200- to 300-year-old firs, hemlocks, and spruces line the path as it travels up and down over six river terraces. The older, higher terraces have the oldest trees; alders, a "pioneering" species, cover the younger terraces made by the deposits of more recent floodways.

Moss-covered maple trees in Big Flat

At about 1 mile the trail drops to Big Flat, the first of the alder-grassy  open areas.

Between 2 and 2½ miles are fenced experimental areas where browsing elk have been excluded since 1979. You'll have to search for them — they are some 50 yards off the trail. The startling contrast between the jungle inside and the open forest outside vividly tells of the enormous amounts of vine maple, salmonberry, currant, fern, and young trees the elk consume. The experimental areas at 2½ miles, immediately to the left of the trail, make a magical picnic area and resting place, with thick moss cushions, fallen logs, enormous old trees, and filtered sunlight playing on the wonderland beauty.

100. Dungeness Spit

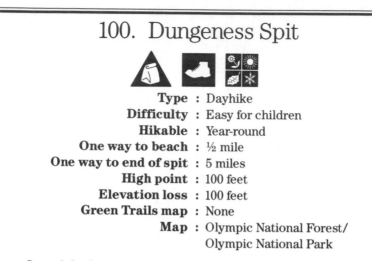

Type	: Dayhike
Difficulty	: Easy for children
Hikable	: Year-round
One way to beach	: ½ mile
One way to end of spit	: 5 miles
High point	: 100 feet
Elevation loss	: 100 feet
Green Trails map	: None
Map	: Olympic National Forest/ Olympic National Park

One of the longest natural sandspits in the United States, Dungeness Spit thrusts out into the Strait of Juan de Fuca. A short descent through forest to the beach leads to its base. The spit is accessible to families at any time of the year; it also attracts harbor seals, killer whales, and bald eagles. The spit reaches far out in the strait, then curves inward like a gigantic arm, with a lighthouse in its "hand." That's a 5-mile walk,

Harbor Seals near Dungeness Spit lighthouse

but there's plenty of fun along the way, and no need to go more than 1 or 2 miles.

Drive U.S. 101 to Sequim. In May and June rhododendrons bloom alongside the highway. From Sequim continue west a little over 2 miles on U.S. 101 to Kitchen–Dick Road, signed "Dungeness Natural Wildlife Refuge." Turn right and drive 3 miles to the road end, right for 1 block on Lotzgesell Road, and left on the Voice of America Road. Go 1 mile to the refuge and continue past the Clallam County campground to the spit parking lot. As of 1988, there is a $2 entrance fee.

The graveled trail wanders ½ mile through forest to a bluff above the Strait of Juan de Fuca, and the first big view of the spit. Drop to the beach and begin the walk on the hard sand of the surf side. Tidal fluctuations will make a difference in the amount of beach exposed.

The beach is as pretty at the start as at the end. The views north are across the water to Vancouver Island with Mount Baker floating above to the northeast, and southwest to the Olympic Mountains. Even a day in total fog, with no view at all, is a mystical experience. Only the sound of foghorns will penetrate the velvet enveloping the spit.

To get away from crowds and for the best chances to see seals, marine birds, and migrating shorebirds, hike some distance. Killer whales, the famous orcas, are unpredictable, but they often swim on the open side of the spit. Harbor seals supplement their fish diet with the eel-grass on the bay side. Older children may want to go the whole 5 miles and climb the steps of the lighthouse tower, built in 1857.

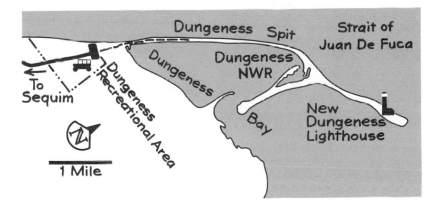

Beachcombing at Deception Pass State Park

Whidbey Island Highway

State Route 20

101. Ebey's Landing...246
102. Deception Pass...248

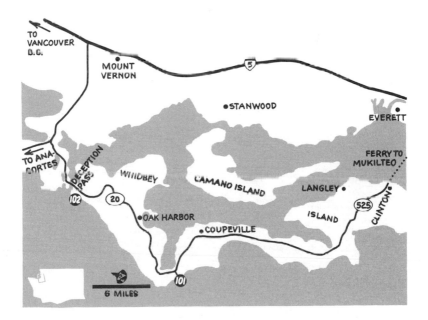

101. Ebey's Landing

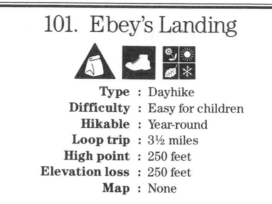

Type : Dayhike
Difficulty : Easy for children
Hikable : Year-round
Loop trip : 3½ miles
High point : 250 feet
Elevation loss : 250 feet
Map : None

In our family the beach of the Ebey's Landing National Historic Preserve is the most beloved of the state's inland sea hikes. My children loved Ebey's Landing for its beauty, its history, and the endless opportunities to play. The trail on the bluff above the beach has some steep portions that are a struggle for toddlers. But once on top, my kids would

Perego's Lagoon

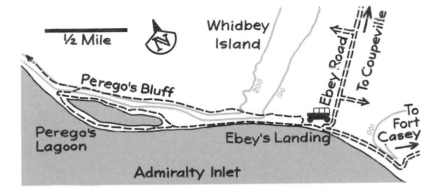

½ Mile

Whidbey Island

Perego's Bluff

Perego's Lagoon

Ebey Road

To Coupeville

To Fort Casey

Ebey's Landing

Admiralty Inlet

gaze entranced down to the long tidal lagoon, west to Port Townsend and the Olympics, and south to Mount Rainier. Ebey's Landing Inn, listed on the National Historic Register, stands back in a field behind a locked gate. It is the old house with the distinctive moss-covered roof and tall chimneys. Colonel Isaac Ebey settled here in 1850 and was murdered and beheaded by raiding Haida Indians in 1857. The inn was built in 1860 and continued to operate until the 1920s. Its plans are on view in the Library of Congress, but it is not open to the public.

Drive Highway 20 from either the north or south end of Whidbey Island. At 0.3 mile north of the Coupeville pedestrian overpass turn left at a power station onto Ebey Road. At 1¾ miles from the highway, drop to a small parking lot at Ebey's Landing.

Those with very young children should walk the beach north 1 mile to Perego's Lagoon and devote the day to waves and driftwood. Families with older children can do a loop, starting either with beach or bluff. We always preferred to begin with the bluff. To do so, walk north from the parking lot and shortly ascend the low bank to a path paralleling the cultivated field. The bank tilts up steeply to become bluff, passing the front edge of a forest of Douglas fir, Sitka spruce, and pines contorted by prevailing winds. Trees lean picturesquely, framing Mount Rainier and the Olympics. The glorious views over table-flat Ebey's Prairie are right out of the 19th century (it's the longest continuously farmed land in the state), include the Strait, and the ocean horizon far beyond. Once atop the bluff, the level path is bordered by wild roses, broom, paintbrush, and wind-groomed salal. At about 1½ miles descend a steep trail to the north end of Perego's Lagoon below, where children can skip rocks and play in the driftwood, watching for loons and seals in the waves. Walk south to your car along a shore offering superb beachcombing. Some years the lagoon has fresh water; in others the banks are breached and the lagoon is tidal. When this happens, the return trip will be on a narrow path along the bluff side of the lagoon.

102. Deception Pass

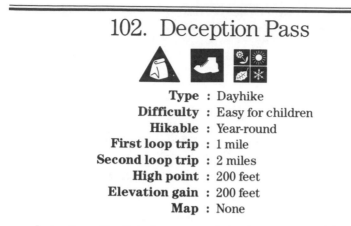

Type	: Dayhike
Difficulty	: Easy for children
Hikable	: Year-round
First loop trip	: 1 mile
Second loop trip	: 2 miles
High point	: 200 feet
Elevation gain	: 200 feet
Map	: None

Lots of sand to shovel, scoop, and play in; a mammoth bridge to gaze up at; eagles to spot; boats to watch; numerous forest trails to explore. Deception Pass is an ideal place to take children for a day, or a weekend, or a week.

Leave I-5 north of Mount Vernon at Exit No. 230 and drive Highway 20 west to Fidalgo Island. On the island follow signs to Deception Pass. Enter Deception State Park at Pass Lake and drive on the Deception Pass Bridge. If you wish, stop on Pass Island to walk out on the bridge and watch the boats below fighting against or going with the strong currents. Then continue on to Whidbey Island and go right into the Deception Pass Park headquarters area to the large parking lot at West Beach.

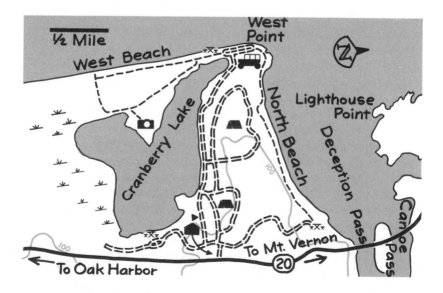

Indian totem at West Beach

There are many trails to explore, but the two described here are my favorites with children. If your children are like mine, they will first head for the sand dunes. On the Cranberry Lake side of the parking lot find the paved trail behind the rest rooms. The trail passes a series of dunes covered with sedge, beach morning glory, and beach pea. A sign marked "Foredunes" describes those closest to the shoreline. Stay on the trail. The vegetation and dunes are too fragile even for little feet. In ¼ mile reach the park boundary. For sand play, turn right and go to the beach. For a 1-mile loop hike, go left past more sand dunes signed "Precipitation Dunes." Climb a wooden platform for an overlook of marshes and tea-colored Cranberry Lake. Yes, wild cranberries grow here — some at the edge of the lake. Another bog plant, Labrador tea, also thrives in this acid soil. (You can recognize it by its small, leathery yellow-green leaves.) Rub a leaf and hold it next to your face for a pungent aroma.

The 2-mile second loop hike begins at the other end of the parking lot and takes the trail over the rocky headland of West Point, then drops to the first beach of North Bay. Expect to see large old Douglas firs framing views of the water, which will probably be filled with sailboats, fishing vessels, and tugboats pulling logs, all waiting until the tide turns and runs in their direction. From the first bay, bear left into woods past a car campground and go about ¼ mile to the next beach. At low tide the beach can be walked. Look up at the bridge and note how small the people standing on it seem. Look still higher for eagles soaring (we saw four one March day) above the water. You can also see scaups, coots, scoters, and all kinds of ducks. Continue ¼ mile to the third beach. At the headland above the third beach, turn right and follow the curving road uphill past park headquarters, then downhill past Cranberry Lake to the parking lot.

Index

Anderson Lake — 32
Ann, Lake — 40
Annette, Lake — 132
Apple Lake — 172
Arbuthnot Lake — 24
Ashland Lakes — 70
Baker River — 34
Barclay Lake — 90
Barlow Point — 78
Beacon Rock — 220
Bear Lake — 215
Beljica, Mount — 181
Benson Basin — 53
Benson Pass — 52
Bertha May Lake — 176
Big Flat — 241
Big Four Ice Caves — 74
Big Four Mountain — 74
Black Lake — 54
Blankenship Lakes — 168
Blankenship Meadows — 169, 173
Blue Creek campground — 116
Blue Lake (Baker River) — 30
Blue Lake (North Cascades) — 46
Boardman Lake — 68
Bolt Camp — 206
Boulder Lake — 86
Boulder River Ford — 59
Boulder River Waterfall — 58
Box Creek — 111
Burroughs Mountain — 158
Butte Camp — 218
Camp Robber Creek — 93
Carbon Glacier — 148
Carbon River Camp — 149
Carne Mountain trail — 111
Cascade Pass — 38
Chain Lakes — 24
Chipmunk Creek — 111
Christine, Lake — 180
Coleman Glacier — 19
Columbia Gorge — 220
Comet Falls — 188
Cottonwood Lake — 139
Council Bluff — 204
Cultus Lake — 215

Curly Creek viewpoint — 207
Cutthroat Lakes — 82
Dee Lake — 213
Deer Lake (Olympic Peninsula) — 234
Deer Lake (White Pass) — 200
Denny Creek Water Slide — 128
Dewey Lakes — 166
Dock Butte — 31
Dorothy, Lake — 92
Doubtful Lake — 39
Dumbbell Lake — 172
Dungeness Spit — 242
    lighthouse — 243
Eagles Roost — 153
Easton Glacier — 28
Ebey's Landing — 246
Ebey's Landing Inn — 246
Eight Mile Lake — 112
Elk Overlook — 231
Emmons Glacier moraine — 154
Entiat River — 118
Eunice Lake (Mount Rainier) — 150
Eunice Lake (South Cascades) — 213
Evan, Lake — 68
Excelsior Mountain — 20
Franklin Falls — 130
French Creek bridge — 115
French Creek Campground — 114
Frozen Lake — 158
Glacier Basin — 154
Goat Lake — 62
Goat Peak — 48
Goat Wall — 48
Government Trail — 79
Grace Lakes — 98
Granite Lake — 176
Grove of the Patriarchs — 196
Happy Four — 239
Harts Pass — 53
Hayes Lake — 24
Heather Creek — 65
Heather Lake
    (Mountain Loop Highway) — 64
Heather Lake (South Cascades) — 213
Heather Lake (Stevens Pass east) — 106
Heather Pass — 42

Heliotrope Ridge — 18
Hidden Lake — 108
Hidden Springs — 199
High Rock — 178
Hoh Rain Forest — 238
Hoh River, South Fork — 240
Humes Ranch — 230
Humpback Creek — 133
Hurricane Hill — 228
Hyas Lakes — 144
Iceberg Lake — 25
Independence Lake — 76
Indian Heaven — 214
Indian Henry's Hunting Ground — 182
Ipsut Creek — 148
Janus, Lake — 39
Kelcema Lake — 72
Kennedy Hot Springs — 60
Klapatche Park — 186
Krause Bottom — 231
Kwaddis, Lake — 213
Lemie Lake — 215
Lena Creek — 227
Lena Lake, Lower — 226
Leroy Creek — 111
Lewis River Trail — 206
Loowit Trail — 218
Mad Lake — 116
Mad River — 116
Maple Pass — 40, 43
Mazama Lake — 25
Michaels Ranch cabin — 231
Milwaukee Railroad grade — 133
Mirror Lake — 138
Mix-Up Arm — 39
Everett & Monte Cristo
  Railroad grade — 79
Monte Cristo Road — 80
Myrtle Lake — 118
Naches Peak — 167
  loop — 164
Ninety-nine Ridge — 50
Norway Pass — 216
Olallie Lake — 126
Olympic Hot Springs — 232
Pacific Crest Trail — 50, 53, 105, 163, 167,
  172, 200, 215
Packwood Lake — 194
Perego's Lagoon — 247
Park Butte — 29
Pear Lake — 172
Penoyer Lake — 172
Pete Lake — 142
Phelps Creek — 110
Pinnacle Saddle — 190
Pothole Lake — 176
Rachel Lake — 140

Railroad Grade — 28
Rampart Ridge — 141
Sahale Arm — 39
Sand Lake — 200
Sauk Mountain — 36
Sawyer Pass — 97
Second Beach — 236
Shadow Lake trail — 156
Sheep Lake — 162
Shellrock Lake — 172
Shoe Lake — 198
Skokomish River — 224
Skyline Lake — 98
Sleeping Beauty — 208
Snow Lake — 134
  Saddle — 135
Soleduck Falls — 234
Sourdough Gap — 163
Spider Meadow — 110
Spray Falls — 153
Spray Park — 152
St. Andrews Lake — 187
Staircase Rapids trail — 225
Steamboat Mountain — 210
Strawberry Bay — 236
Sulphide Creek — 35
Sunrise Camp — 158
Tahoma Creek — 182
Talapus Lake — 126
Tatie Pass — 50
Taylor Head — 237
Thomas Lake — 213
Tiger Mountain, Middle — 124
Tipsoo Lakes — 165
Tolmie Peak lookout — 150
Tom Creek trail — 230
Tonga Ridge — 96
Tradition Lake — 122
  Plateau — 122
Trout Lake — 94
Tumac Mountain — 169, 170
Twenty-two, Lake — 66
Twin Lakes — 22
Twin Sisters Lakes — 168, 170
  Big — 170
  Little — 170, 172
Union Gap — 105
Valhalla, Lake — 100
Van Trump Park — 188
Wallace Falls — 88
Watson Lake — 32
William O. Douglas
  Wilderness — 172
Winchester Mountain — 22
Windy Pass — 53
Wonderland Trail — 150, 187
Woody Trail — 89

About the author:

Seattle resident Joan Burton was herself introduced to hiking as a child, and by the time she had reached her teens, had climbed the six highest mountains in Washington. Later, as a parent with growing children she was involved in introducing not only her own family to the joys of outdooring, but also members of the Girl Scout and Cub Scout groups of which she was leader. Burton is a long-time member of The Mountaineers, and a graduate of both the basic and intermediate climbing courses taught by that club. After a number of years teaching high school English, Burton is now an editorial assistant on an academic medical journal. She has published several magazine articles on outdoor subjects; this is her first book.